3 minute
DISCOURSES
on Kabbalah by Leading
JEWISH SCHOLARS

3minute
DISCOURSES
on Kabbalah by Leading
JEWISH SCHOLARS

JASON ARONSON INC.
Northvale, New Jersey
Jerusalem

Illustrations on page 28 from *The Encyclopedia of Jewish Symbols*, by Ellen Frankel and Betsy Platkin Teutsch. © 1992.

This book was set in 12 pt. Garamond Book by Alabama Book Composition of Deatsville, AL and printed and bound by Book-mart Press, Inc. of North Bergen, NJ.

Library of Congress Cataloging-in-Publication Data

3-minute discourses on kabbalah by the world's leading scholars

      p. cm.
     Includes bibliographical references and index.
     ISBN 0-7657-6194-7
     1. Cabala—History. 2. Mysticism—Judaism. 3. Meditation—Judaism. I. Title: Three-minute discourses on kabbalah by the world's leading scholars.

BM526 .A13   2001
293.1'6—dc21

                                              00-069993

Printed in the United States of America on acid-free paper. For information and catalog, write to Jason Aronson Inc., 230 Livingston Street, Northvale, NJ 07647-1726, or visit our website: www.aronson.com

Contents

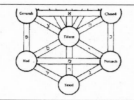
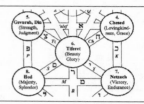
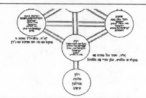

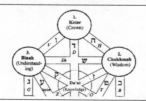

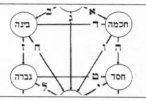
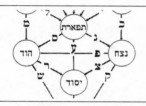
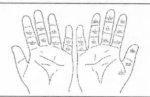

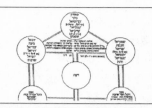

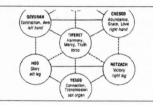
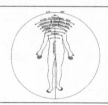

Preface

Rabbi Adin Steinsaltz, internationally regarded as one of the leading rabbis of our time and well-known for his books and lectures on Jewish mystical thought, was once asked if it is permissible for the novice to study Kabbalah. He replied, "The question is not who is learning Kabbalah; the question is who is teaching it?"

One need only browse the shelves of a bookstore (in both the Judaica and the "New Age" sections) or listen to the media to know that Kabbalah is a popular subject these days. From Hollywood personalities to local adult education classes, the interest in Kabbalah is clearly on the rise.

For many centuries, the study of Kabbalah has been available to very few. The English word *cabal*, derived from the word *Kabbalah*, means a "secret society," pointing to the fact that Kabbalah has, for a long time, been considered a subject for a small number of individuals. Today, with the ease of communication, and with the mass distribution of books as a result of the phenomenon of the Internet, it is common for there to be widespread dissemination of information — as well as misinformation — seemingly on every subject.

3 Minute Discourses on Kabbalah by Leading Jewish Scholars gathers the writings of leading scholars in the field. Its goal is to introduce the basic ideas of Kabbalah to those who desire reliable information and insight into Jewish mystical tradition. These discourses, taken from some of the most important books on Kabbalah available today, also serve to point the serious student of Kabbalah to sources and resources that are essential for further study.

I
The Jewish Mystical Tradition

1

Mysticism in the Jewish Tradition

Adin Steinsaltz

Jewish mysticism never really became a separate domain of spiritual life outside the religious tradition.
This may be due to the fact that the initial revelation at
Mount Sinai was holy in such a way that it could never
be shaken off. The Torah scriptures, at all levels of their
composition, from the Bible to the Talmud and the
latest commentaries of the sages, succeeded in retain-
ing and elaborating this experience so profoundly that
there was not much room for an emotional mysticism,
either private or cultic, to develop on its own, outside
of the established religious form.

Nevertheless, at a certain stage in Jewish history
(from about the seventeenth century), the religious
authorities believed that there was a significant danger
in that direction. And in Europe at least, Kabbalah, the

chief repository of the mystical aspect of the tradition, was taken firmly in hand. Only mature students were permitted to study it, and carefully preserved texts were left to gather dust and sink into oblivion. In later years (mostly in the nineteenth century) there was another, newer element that helped to suppress the mystical lore. Within the strong rationalistic tendency of the age, many influential people (such as the authors of the most important books of Jewish history) were fiercely antagonistic to any mystical approach and tried to disparage it and even deny its existence in the past. The apologetic mood of the time demanded hiding these shameful parts of Judaism and trying to forget them entirely. The result has been a general misunderstanding of the role of the Kabbalah, and of the mystical experience altogether in Judaism.

The truth is that the Kabbalah permeates every

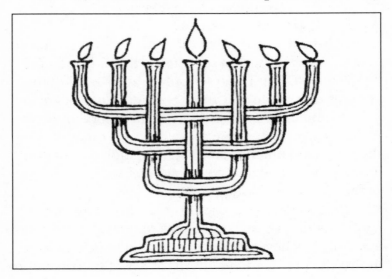

aspect of Judaism, and the "esoteric wisdom" has been a basic ingredient of scripture, ritual, and prayer. Even

---

The Kabbalah permeates every aspect of Judaism, and the "esoteric wisdom" has been a basic ingredient of scripture, ritual, and prayer.

---

many popular expressions, in Hebrew but also in the colloquial Yiddish, have their source in the Kabbalah.

Although a careful distinction was maintained throughout these centuries between the *nigleh* and the *nistar*, between the revealed and the hidden aspects of the religion, it was never a division within the people or within Judaism as conceived by its greatest authorities. The *Shulhan Arukh*, the great work that has become the fundamental halakhic text for all of Jewry, was written by Rabbi Joseph Caro, a sage whose authority rested not only on his very broad learning but also on his many-sidedness and mystic insight. He wrote other books of halakhic procedure and law, exegeses on Torah and the like, and in addition he wrote a treatise called *Maggid M'esharim*, which was certainly a kabbalistic work and showed him to be a man who had mystical experiences and visions. Those of his generation who heard about his revelations were inclined to say that it was the voice of the *Mishnah* speaking from his mouth. To this day, the inspired orders of prayers we follow on the all-night *tikkun* of Shavuot are those of Rabbi Joseph Caro. And one of his closest disciples wrote the famous *Shabbat* song "*Lechah Dodi*," now accepted in all circles of Jewish worship, which is obviously a kabbalistic poem.

So we see that the greatest of the halakhic legal authorities was very much immersed in the mystical world
of Kabbalah.

An interesting item in Rabbi Joseph Caro's biogra-
phy is that he was a contemporary of the Holy Ari,
Rabbi Isaac Luria. The two even lived in the same city of
Safed. The Ari was the greatest kabbalist luminary,
according to whom the Kabbalah was crystallized into
its recognized final forms. The Ari wrote hardly anything himself; his teachings were transmitted orally, as
were most ancient traditions. We have three short
poems from his pen, as well as a legal commentary on
a tractate of the Talmud.

~

All of this is only to indicate that there was never a
separation of any real consequence between the daily
obligations and open practice of Judaism and the esoteric or mystical aspects of the tradition. They have
always been connected. They are simply different aspects of the same thing. In the Middle Ages many
scholars leaned almost entirely on the writings of Maimonides and pointed to his Thirteen Articles of Faith as
the supreme theological authority. But even in those
times there was more than one approach to theology.
For example, we also have the more mystical approach
of Rabbi Moshe ben Nachman (the Ramban). But since
there was no central authority to define a consensus of
opinion, the differences — which, as intimated, were
never as polarized as modern thinkers believe — were
allowed to flourish. It is only since the sixteenth century that there has been a consensus accepted by

almost every Jew. If there is a normative Jewish theology, it is the integration of the two (never really separate) approaches—the Kabbalah of the Ari and the
Shulhan Arukh of Rabbi Joseph Caro.

This was possible because unlike most mystical
schools in the world, which somehow stressed their
freedom from the constraints of formal religion (even
when they continued to remain within it), Kabbalah
mysticism did the opposite. It always stressed the vital
significance of the smallest details of the law and the

---

*Unlike most mystical schools in the world, which
somehow stressed their freedom from the
constraints of formal religion (even when they
continued to remain within it), Kabbalah
mysticism did the opposite.*

---

ritual. The kabbalists even added weight and meaning
to the formal practices in a thousand ways. And when it
came to such issues of theoretical theology as the
Thirteen Articles of Faith, they simply put different
emphasis on the same words. To be sure, they had their
disagreements with some of Maimonides' ideas; nevertheless, they did not let disagreement develop into
friction and antagonism. Everything in the tradition
was somehow incorporated into the kabbalistic framework with a certain broad spiritual comprehensive-
ness. What is astonishing, at least to the rational thinking
of the Western world, is that there were no great contradictions, that the two modes of religiosity worked
together as well as they did.

All the Jewish scholars who achieved any degree of

eminence were involved in every world of Torah. The Torah was never considered merely knowledge — as that which one learns with the mind and in which one becomes an expert. As one of the sages, Hillel Zeitlin, said: "In many religions there is the notion of a book or doctrine that comes from heaven. We Jews, however, believe that the Torah itself is heaven." When one is studying the Torah, one is in direct communion with

---

*When one is studying the Torah, one is in
direct communion with God.*

God. One is not just reading or studying or even seeking inspiration. In Judaism we, God and man, are talking together. As it is written in the *Zohar*: there are three things that are connected with each other — the Jews with the Torah, and the Torah with God. We do not delve into the Torah just in order to know something in our past or to learn how to behave. To be engaged with Torah is not just the fulfillment of a commandment, a *mitzvah*; it is in itself being as close to the Almighty as we will ever be.

In the *Pirkei Avot* ("Sayings of the Fathers"), a familiar tractate of the *Mishnah*, there is a statement to the effect that one hour of happiness in the world to come is better than all the life of this world. Such a belief may satisfy the mystical ardor of many religious people. But this statement is followed by another — a very baffling opposite to the first — declaring that one hour of *teshuvah* (repentance) and *maasim tovim* (good deeds) in this world is worth more than all the life in the world to come. This is to say that we, in this world, have something no other world contains: we can come into direct communion with God through his Torah. When we study Scripture, God studies with us, the Talmud says. When we perform actions according to the Torah, we are not separate from Him.

Learning is therefore not just an intellectual tie; the more one understands, the more one is connected. Understanding requires a lot of discipline, of the emotions as well as of the mind. The intensity of all thought and feeling has to be contained and directed. Therefore, too, the Torah has its many parts, allowing for a healthy organic life within the tradition. But as with anything of such an organic wholeness, the parts are also interdependent. A faulty part can put the whole thing in danger of breakdown. If the whole thing is, like one of the modern rockets, a vehicle to heaven, a flaw in any one small component can prove disastrous indeed.

Evidently, then, all the parts of the Torah are essential. They are not just complementary or supportive of each other; they also use different means, different languages, to say the same thing, whether it is *Halakhah* or *Kabbalah*, *Mishnah* or *Zohar*. For example, the prayer book has this formula for performing a *mitzvah*: "To unite the Holy One, blessed be He, and the *Shekhinah*." This is a kabbalistic formula. And it signifies that this union of Divine manifestation is the same single purpose of all our actions, no matter which of the *mitzvot* are involved. The scope of the Torah is always beyond any of its parts. It is always the same and it is possible to approach it, to view it, from many different angles.

Customarily, we speak of the different ways of dealing with Torah, from the explicit to the implicit, from *peshat*(literal meaning) to *derash* (exegesis), to *remez* (hint), to *sod* (secret or esoteric truth). All these simply address the same words of Scripture in four different languages, all of which have the same meaning. One of the methods of study is to gain an understanding of the way these languages change from one form of expression to another, how they change from saying something in poetic terms to those of a story, a commandment, and a kabbalistic idea. Consequently, the common view about mysticism and Kabbalah being a different world from the Talmud is a misconception of the organic unity of the whole. The Kabbalah

---

The common view about mysticism and Kabbalah being a different world from the Talmud is a misconception of the organic unity of the whole.

---

and the Talmud are different forms of expression, each following its own point of departure.

~

As mentioned, the religious authorities had their historical reasons—like the tragic event of the false Messiah, Shabbetai Tzvi—for frowning on the study of Kabbalah. On the other hand, there can be no denying the perils of the esoteric and the occult. The common people were simply advised to keep away from subjects they did not know enough about, a little knowledge being a dangerous thing in any field. And as far as Torah is concerned, since it is a live wire connecting us with God, anyone who gets involved without taking precautionary measures runs the risk of being electrocuted.

It was in this sense that Kabbalah used to be considered a field that was not accessible to all. There was a need for special knowledge and sensitivity to be able to enter into the realm of the hidden. When studying the Talmud, it is all too apparent when one does not quite comprehend a passage, because the Talmud speaks about people, animals, the mundane affairs of men. A student can easily discern what he grasps and what he does not. But when studying the Kabbalah — which speaks about *sefirot*, angels, Divine lights, and vessels — the ability to distinguish one's own lack of understanding is far more difficult, so that the subtle danger of misconception is a sad inevitability accompanying such study. All of this is not intended to divert attention from the fact that the Torah, including the manifest and the hidden, is all one. To be sure, it is said

---

The Torah has so many locks and keys, and each key is individual, each doorway is one's own.

---

that it has seventy faces. Indeed, some sources say it has six hundred thousand faces, because that is the number of souls who received the Torah when it was revealed, and each one has, to this day, his own understanding of it, his own orientation and point of view.

When we pray, saying "Give us our portion in your Torah," it is to let us have the merit and the good fortune to grasp our own private portion of the Torah. For the Torah has so many locks and keys, and each key is individual, each doorway is one's own. A person can be considered very fortunate if he finds the special key, the private door that is his to enter. Too often people just keep wandering about getting involved with other people's keys and doors; they make mistakes and get themselves confused and entangled in points of view not their own. The simplest solution is to be certain that one's connection to Torah exists. If one just lets attention be properly oriented, it is possible to feel that certain sentences in prayer, certain passages of Scripture, have special appeal to oneself; they speak to one. Many Jews will learn these passages by heart, becoming emotionally intimate with certain words that serve them as a doorway.

The same thing is true of commandments. Of course, it is required that the whole Torah be accepted and no exceptions be made. Nevertheless, every individual should take at least one *mitzvah* as a very special commandment to be performed with a sense of particular satisfaction and inner happiness. When, in the Talmud, Rav Yosef asks the son of Raba: "What commandment was your father most particular about?" he is inquiring not only which commandment he kept most meticulously, but also which was most important to him.

In another book, the word meaning observant, careful, particular also means to shine. So that the Talmud question reads: In which *mitzvah* did your father feel most of the light? Sometimes there is something that passes before one like a flash of lightning or a resplendent illumination that lights up one's way. It is that key to Torah that is yours, your way, that speaks to you.

Some people find this key in the realm of intellectual content. Others, in the doing of certain actions, the performance of *mitzvot*, and this has as much meaning for them as the complex idea of the intellectual or mystical experiences of the kabbalist. All lead to the inner chambers of the Divine presence. The point is that for each seeker such a key is the hidden secret of one's destiny; beyond rational explanation, it remains beautiful and personally meaningful for a significant period of time if not for all of one's life. The other side of the same truth is that each one is expressing the same thing, the same melody in six hundred thousand voices. For every person has his own unique voice, even when the song is the same.

If a person is unsure of himself, and wishes to know whether his way is appropriate to him, one of the tests of validity would be to examine its flexibility — whether it can be translated into different levels of the hidden or the manifest, as the case may be. It should lend itself with ease to a variety of expressions. If this cannot be done, if his key cannot open the whole of Torah, it may be necessary to reexamine that key and see if it is not perhaps a delusion. There should be more than one way of getting to any problem of truth. A problem, whether it concerns mathematics or science or spiritual reality, can usually be solved in more than one way. What is essential is that all the approaches should lead to the same correct solution. Some go through the air, some by sea, others over land. All should lead to an equivalent answer, even if couched in different words, even if they sound oddly at variance.

Thus the mystical contents of Kabbalah are not

necessarily restricted to *sefirot* and angels and other-
worldly forces; they are also in the familiar constituents

---

*For some people the most revealed of Torah
passages is full of secret meaning and wrapped
in unfathomable mystery; for others, even the
most esoteric wisdom is bright and clear,
with nothing mysterious about it.*

---

and motions of the body, in the Bible and the Talmud,
in all the many vehicles of the Torah. To be sure, the
truth cannot be found in the wrongness of things, in
the hidden evil, no matter how deliciously secret, or in
any myster that is at once confounding and soluble.
Mystery or mystical experience may simply be the way
one sees certain truths. For some people the most
revealed of Torah passages is full of secret meaning and
wrapped in unfathomable mystery; for others, even the
most esoteric wisdom is bright and clear, with nothing
mysterious about it. The Baal Shem Tov used to say:
The numerical value of *sod* (secret) is exactly that of *or*
(light).

All of this is best summarized by the story Rabbi
Shimshon of Ostropol, who is famous for his two books
on Kabbalah. It is told that he decided one day to write
a complete kabbalistic commentary on the Talmud, to
explain the secret and hidden meanings of this enormous body of Jewish learning. He made good use of
his knowledge of esoteric wisdom and completed the
complex work after considerable labor. But being a
very holy man, he subjected the book to the test of a
dream, *she'eilat halom*, and the answer he got to his

questions was that his work was too lengthy and elaborate. He made it shorter and again posed the question. The answer was the same: too long. Again he cut his work down, and again he was told that it was not sufficiently precise and clear. When he had made it as short and concise as he could, he discovered that what he had written was *Perush Rashi*, the accepted commentary on the Talmud.

From *On Being Free*.

Rabbi Adin Steinsaltz, scholar, teacher, mystic, scientist, and social critic, is internationally regarded as one of the leading rabbis of this century. The author of many books, he is best known for his monumental translation of and commentary on the Talmud. In 1988, Rabbi Steinsaltz was awarded the Israel Prize, his country's highest honor. He and his family live in Jerusalem.

2

Interpreting
Kabbalistic Imagery

Donald Wilder Menzi and Zwe Padeh

How are we to interpret this complex, richly anthro-pomorphic kabbalistic imagery? For the kabbalist, the structure of the ten *sefirot* provides a conceptual framework for understanding God's interaction with the world, viewed as an ongoing creative process in which we are active partners. One may legitimately ask, however, What is the practical relevance of a concept such as the *sefirot* to the contemporary world of everyday experience?

To anyone involved in creative activity, the process can, in fact, seem like a constant interplay between generating and limiting forces, in which one moves from the abstract to the concrete in a succession of stages that seem to parallel the structure of the *sefirot*.

Inspiration, conceptualization, a period of development, testing, criticism, correction, production, modification, the achievement of excellence, and the transfer of what has been learned to new realms of endeavor—all can be found in almost any creative process, whether it be writing a book or a play, designing an automobile, or one's own life.

Viewing the creative process through the lens of the *sefirot* can provide a new perspective on many of our "negative" experiences—criticism, rejection, bad reviews, the discovery of mistakes—enabling them to be seen as aspects of the creative process that can make important, if sometimes painful, contributions to an ultimately positive outcome.

With regard to the *partzufim* and other forms of anthropomorphism—the use of human images to describe spiritual realities—it is useful to remember that

much religious language is symbolic, an attempt to put into words a reality that has been experienced but can be described only by analogy. *Etz Chayyim* repeatedly states that there are no vessels or letters or any bodily aspects in the higher realms, only "pure light, utterly spiritual, which cannot be grasped at all" (p. 54). The use of anthropomorphic language in speaking of the divine realm is, however, common in the Bible. It occurs to a lesser extent in the Talmud, but becomes especially pronounced in the *Zohar*, which kabbalists consider to be nearly equal to the Bible and the Talmud in its holiness. Isaac Luria continued that tradition, focusing especially on the love between man and woman as the dominant metaphor for describing the relationship between the human and the divine, and between the various aspects of divinity itself. In so doing, he equates this most intimate of human relationships with the deepest of truths about the universe.

The kabbalistic view that all existence is a constant interplay between the outwardly visible world and an unseen realm hidden just beneath its surface, encourages intense engagement, conscious intention, and mindfulness in every human act since, from this perspective, even seemingly unimportant events may potentially have cosmic significance.

The Lurianic concept of *tikkun* (correction) was originally applied to the primordial reconfiguration of the *sefirot* into *partzufim*, to our actions in liberating and restoring to their source the hidden sparks of holiness scattered throughout the world, and to the individual's progressive advance toward spiritual perfection through successive incarnations. Today, this

term is used to express the thoroughly modern concept of improving the world — *tikkun 'olam* — in all
its aspects.

For those who are used to thinking of God only as a
single, undivided Supreme Being, the ten *sefirot* of the
Kabbalah — much less their personification as a family
of *partzufim* — may seem difficult to reconcile with
Judaism's traditionally strict monotheism. Yet the classical kabbalists continued to follow traditional Jewish
religious practices and strongly asserted their belief in
God's unity. The *Zohar* contains many different images

---

*For those who are used to thinking of God only
as a single, undivided Supreme Being, the ten
sefirot of the Kabbalah — much less their
personification as a family of partzufim — may
seem difficult to reconcile with Judaism's
traditionally strict monotheism.*

---

and analogies that illustrate the theme of unity beneath
the diversity of the *sefirot*, and *Etz Chayyim* repeatedly
identifies the individual *sefirot* and *partzufim* as aspects of a larger whole. The highest Divine Name itself
is a single word whose individual letters — counting
the tip of the *yod* separately — correspond to the five
partzufim, which are themselves a reconfiguration of
the ten *sefirot*. And in all the kabbalistic writings the
Infinite — both surrounding and hidden deep within
a multifaceted reality — is ultimately the single, undivided source of them all.

But if the kabbalist's God is ultimately singular, our
experience of this God calls for a complex, rather than

a simple, form of monotheism. In Lurianic Kabbalah, the unity of the unseen realms — the intermediate levels between our finite universe and the undivided Infinite — is broken, and this broken-ness is reflected in our experience of this world as out-of-joint, incomplete, fragmentary, and unbalanced. The imbalance and disharmony so often present between male and female; between parent and child; between the diverse cultures, classes, and races of humankind; between religions and between religious denominations; between humans and their environment; and even between the various aspects of our own personalities are evidence of this underlying lack of unity. The ideal solution to the broken-ness of this world lies, for the kabbalist, not in the imposition of a homogeneous uniformity, but in recognizing a dynamic diversity in which the seemingly disparate parts are seen as aspects of a greater whole. We participate in the unfinished task of bringing about this wholeness as partners with God in the ongoing redemptive process of *tikkun 'olam* — repairing the universe — by seeking out the sparks of holiness hidden in this world among the broken Shells of evil, elevating them through prayer, *mitzvot*, and deeds of kindness to reveal God's presence in every detail of our earthly existence, thus unifying the upper and the lower worlds. And only when the work of cosmic unification is finished will "the Lord be one, and His Name be one" (Zechariah 14:9), not only in the theoretical formulations of our monotheistic theologies but at all levels of existence, seen and unseen.

Kabbalah is sometimes referred to as "Jewish mys-

ticism," but to call Kabbalah "mysticism" is misleading,
at best. Kabbalah is not primarily about "the intuitive
and emotive apprehension of reality." While its imagery — its "clothing," in the language of the Kabbalah
itself may sound strange to modern ears, the religious
philosophy and world-view embodied within these
images have important things to say to us. Even when it
speaks of "higher" spiritual realms, it is usually referring not to something "up there," high above us, but
"down here," deep within us. Its literature includes a
number of treatises on personal morality and ethical

---

*Kabbalah is sometimes referred to as
"Jewish mysticism," but to call Kabbalah
"mysticism" is misleading, at best.*

---

behavior. Its complexity mirrors the complexity of life
itself. Its techniques combine traditional teachings, dramatic metaphor, logical analysis, and inference from
the intimately familiar to the ultimately unknowable.
Its canvas is large, extending beyond the outermost
limits of time and space and the innermost levels of the
soul. Yet its rigorous logic and internal consistency
assure us that everything is ultimately related to everything else, and that there is an underlying order and
unity, sometimes visible but often hidden from our
eyes, at the heart of the universe. It affirms that even
though all that we can possibly know and do in our
lifetime may seem to us like a speck of dust in an
infinite range of possibilities, none of our efforts for
good in this world are wasted, for each of us has an

important role to play in helping to determine the ultimate fate of the universe.

In Judaism, as in many other traditions, the path to enlightenment includes the study of sacred texts, internalizing and interpreting their meaning for daily life. *Etz Chayyim* — long accessible only to an inner circle who could master its linguistic and conceptual intricacies — belongs with the Bible, the Talmud, and the *Zohar* as one of those sacred texts.

From *The Tree of Life: Chayyim Vital's Introduction to the Kabbalah of Isaac Luria.*

Donald Wilder Menzi, a graduate of Oberlin College, studied Semitic languages, Bible, and Rabbinic literature at Hebrew Union College under a Levi A. Olan Fellowship from 1963 to 1967. He holds Master's degrees in Sacred Theology from Rochester Eastman Theological School (Bexley Hall) and in Urban Planning from Hunter College, as well as a Ph.D. in Public Administration from New York University. He has served as President of West End Synagogue, a Reconstructionist Congregation in New York City. He was first introduced to Kabbalah by Rabbi Salomon Friedlander, *z"l* the Lisker Rebbe, in the early 1970s.

Zwe Padeh attended Yeshivas in Israel before settling in the United States. He has studied Kabbalah for over ten years both at the Kabbalah Center and as a private student of Rav Gideon Lipovsky. Mr. Padeh is a devoted follower of Rabbi Shlomo Carlebach, *z"l*, and founded the Carlebach Yeshiva with Reb Shlomo. Currently he serves as Dean of the Yeshiva and is involved in Jewish outreach work.

II
The History
of Kabbalah

3

A Time-line of
Jewish Mysticism

Sanford L. Drob

**Some Important Dates
in the History of Jewish Mysticism**

Historical Phase	Original Source
Prophetic Judaism	eighth to sixth centuries B.C.E. Isaiah, Ezekiel, and Zechariah
Apocalyptic Judaism	third to second centuries B.C.E. I Enoch, Book of Daniel
Rabbinic Mysticism	c. first century C.E. Johanan Ben Zakkai and his disciples Early Christian Jewish Mystics

Some Important Dates
in the History of Jewish Mysticism

Historical Phase	Original Source
Merkaveh/ Hekhalot Mysticism	first to second century C.E. Book of Enoch, *Hekhalot Rabbatai* (The Greater Palaces), *Hekhalot Zutari* (The Lesser Palaces), and *Merkaveh Rabbah* (The Great Chariot)
	prior to the sixth century C.E. *Shi'r Koma* (Measure of the Body)
Pre- or proto-Kabbalistic Thought	third to the sixth century C.E. *Sefer Yetzirah* (The Book of Formation)

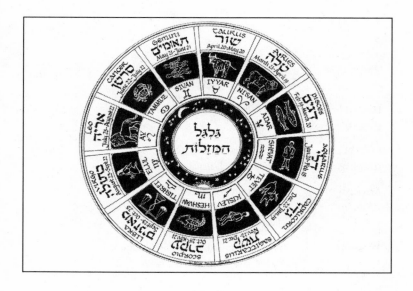

The Early Kabbalah	c. 1175–1200 C.E. *Sefer ha-Bahir* (The Book of Illumination)
	c. 1175–1200 C.E. School of Isaac The Blind
Hasidai Askenaz	Early thirteenth century C.E. Eleazar of Worms
Scholarship	Early thirteenth century C.E. The School of Gerona Azriel of Gerona, Ezra ben Solomon, Jacob ben Sheshet, Moses ben Nachman (Nachmanides)
Zohar	c. 1286, *Sefer ha-Zohar* (The Book of Splendor) is distributed by Moses deLeon, d. 1305. Traditionally attributed to Shimon bar Yochai (second century C.E.). More recently attributed to deLeon and his circle in thirteenth-century Spain.
	c. 1290, Joseph Gikatilla (1284–1325), *Sha'are Orah* (Gates of Light).
Christian Kabbalah	1517 Johannes Reuchlin (1455–1522) publishes *De Arte Cabalistica*, an early work of the Christian Kabbalah.
Safedian Kabbalists	c. 1550, Moses Cordovero (1522–1570), *Pardes Rimmonim* (The Orchard of Pomegranates), Safed.
Lurianic Kabbalah	c. 1569 Isaac Luria (1534–1572) arrives and begins teaching in Safed.
	c. 1620, Chayyim Vital's (1542–1640) works, including those that will later be edited as *Sefer Etz Chayyim*, begin to circulate in manuscript form.

Some Important Dates
in the History of Jewish Mysticism

Historical Phase	Original Source
	1666, Sabbatai Sevi (1626–1676) a Lurianic Kabbalist from Smyrna, and his "prophet" Nathan of Gaza, declare Sabbatai to be the Messiah.
	1730s, Moses Chayyim Luzzatto (1707–1746) writes *Kelah Pithei Chochmah*, a succinct outline of Lurianic Kabbalah.
Chasidism	1760, (d. 1772) Dov Baer of Mezhirech assumes leadership of early Hasidic movement after the death of the Baal Shem Tov. Author of *Maggid Devarev le-Ya'aqov*.
	1797 Schneur Zalman of Lyadi (1745–1813), the first Lubavitcher rebbe (Chabad) publishes *Likutei Amarim — Tanya*.
	1821 Aharon Halevi Horowitz of Staroselye (1766–1828), Chabad theorist, publishes *Sha'arei ha-Avodah* (Gates of Worship).
Jewish Scholarship	1941 Gershom Scholem publishes his *Major Trends In Jewish Mysticism*.

From *Kabbalistic Metaphors: Jewish Mystical Themes in Ancient and Modern Thought*.

Sanford L. Drob is Director of Psychological Assessment and the Senior Forensic Psychologist at Bellevue Hospital in New York. He holds doctorate degrees in Philosophy from Boston University and in Clinical Psychology from Long Island University. In 1987 he co-founded, and for several years served as editor-in-chief of, the *New York Jewish Review*, a publication addressing the interface between traditional Judaism and contemporary thought.

4

The Development
of the Kabbalah

Sanford L. Drob

Table 1 presents an outline of the important dates in
the history of Jewish mysticism. According to contemporary scholarship, the Kabbalah evolved out of
the mixture of the *Merkaveh* mysticism and Neopla-
tonism that dominated Jewish religious speculation
during the early centuries of the Common Era. However, Jewish mysticism itself has its roots in the biblical
tradition. For example, we find as early as Exodus

*Jewish mysticism itself has its roots in the
biblical tradition.*

24:10, a description of God's abode that is relevant to
the development of the kabbalistic doctrine of the

Sefirot: "And they saw the God of Israel: and there was under his feet as it were a paved work of a sapphire (*Sapir*) stone, and as it were the body of heaven in his clearness." The earliest kabbalistic text, *Sefer ha-Bahir*, suggests an etymology of the term *Sefirah* in the Hebrew word for Sapphire (*Sapir*), reinterpreting the Psalm (19:2), "The heavens declare the glory of God" as "the heavens are radiant in the sapphirine radiance of the glory of God."

In the Book of I Kings (22:19) and in the prophet Isaiah (e.g., 6:1-3) we find descriptions of the Lord resplendent on His throne and attended by His hosts, who fill the world with His praise. Such descriptions of the heavenly throne played an important role in the prophetic literature of the eighth to sixth centuries B.C.E. Descriptions of the seraphim and other heavenly beings in the "likeness of a man" (Ezekiel (I:4-28)

ב	פ	ו	ח	כ	מ	י	ו
ו	ב	פ	ו	ח	כ	מ	י
י	ו	ב	פ	ו	ח	כ	מ
מ	י	ו	ב	פ	ו	ח	כ
כ	מ	י	ו	ב	פ	ו	ח
ח	כ	מ	י	ו	ב	פ	ו
ו	ח	כ	מ	י	ו	ב	פ
פ	ו	ח	כ	מ	י	ו	ב

not only had a direct impact upon the *Merkaveh* (chariot) mysticism of the early centuries of the common era, but provided proof-texts for later kabbalistic speculations.

Verman has distinguished among four periods of early Jewish mysticism. The first, which extended from the eighth to the sixth centuries B.C.E., was the era of visionary experience, evident in the prophets *Isaiah*, *Ezekiel*, and *Zechariah*. The second period begins with the end of the Babylonian exile in the sixth century B.C.E., and reaches a high point in the third and second centuries B.C.E. During this period we see a growth in angelology, speculation on the origins of the universe and the creation of man, talk about the "end of days," and descriptions of the afterlife. Such mystical and apocalyptic themes are evident in the book of Daniel and first book of Enoch.

The third period of early Jewish mysticism reaches an apex in the middle of the first century C.E., and is evident not only in Jewish sources but also in the writings of the Christian Jew, Paul, and in the revelation of St. John. According to Verman the mystical ideas attributed to such Mishnaic teachers as Johanan ben Zakkai, Eliezer ben Hyrkanos, Akiva ben Joseph, and Ishmael, the "High Priest," belong to the same tradition of speculation as those of the early Christians. While mystical themes were certainly entertained by the rabbis of this period, the compiler of the Mishnah, Rabbi Judah, made every effort to exclude them, and they are therefore far more apparent in the *Tosefta*, a second mishnaic collection from this same period. The rabbis of the mishnaic and talmudic periods were reluctant to discuss mystical themes in public or commit them to writing. They held that there was a serious danger associated with mystical activity. In Tractate *Chagigah* 14b we find this famous warning:

> Our rabbis taught: Four men entered the garden, namely Ben Azzai and Ben Zoma, Acher and R. Akiba. R. Akiba said to them: When you arrive at the stones of pure marble, say not: Water, water. For it is said: He that speaketh falsehood shall not be established before mine eyes (Psalms 101:7). Ben Azzai cast a look and died. Of him Scripture says: Precious in the eyes of the Lord is the death of His saints (Psalms 116:15). Ben Zoma looked and became demented. Of him Scripture says: Hast thou found honey? Eat as much as is sufficient for thee, lest thou be filled therewith and vomit it (Proverbs 25:16). Acher mutilated the shoots [i.e., brought about heresy]. [Only] R. Akiba went up unhurt, and went down unhurt.

~

While the Talmud is virtually silent on the nature of the mystic's visions of ascent, other contemporary texts provide detailed accounts of these matters. The major extant texts belonging to the period of *Merkaveh* or *Hekhalot* (Palaces) mysticism probably date from the first and second centuries c.e. However, they reflect traditions that are at least two centuries older. Among the literary legacy of this period are the (Jewish) *Book of Enoch*, *Hekhalot Rabbati* (The Greater Palaces),

Hekhalot Zutari (The Lesser Palaces), and *Merkaveh Rabbah* (The Great Chariot). These texts, which are variously said to show the influence of Greek, Persian, and Gnostic themes, treat of the splendor, beauty, and transcendence of God, who reposes on a celestial throne, attended by His heavenly hosts who sing His praise. Here we learn of the *yored merkaveh*, the spiritual adept who ascends (literally and paradoxically "descends") on the chariot, through the seven gates, past the gatekeeping angels who attempt to deter him with fantastic and terrifying illusions, to a vision of the throne and the countenance of God Himself. Numerous angels are here described; in the *Book of Enoch* seven angelic princes are said to be in charge of the seven heavens, and the angel Metatron is the attendant to the throne, and the intermediary between God and the world. We learn that Metatron receives a "crown" on which God, with a finger like a flaming stylus, engraves the letters of creation. This notion of God engraving the letters of creation will later play an important role in both *Sefer Yetzirah* and the Zohar.

In *Hekhalot Zutari* we also see, in anticipation of later kabbalistic themes, an emphasis on the theurgic and magical power of divine names. The "transmission of the mystery" in *Merkaveh Rabbah* is indeed a mystical knowledge of God's names. Further, in these works there is a description of divine robes or garments, the vision of which, according to *Hekhalot Rabbati*, is the goal of the mystical adept. In the Kabbalah divine "garments" become an important metaphor for the *Sefirot*. Finally, in this literature we find a development of the rabbinic theme that God is mysti-

cally dependent upon man's liturgical praise, an idea
that anticipates the Zohar's dictum that man can be
said to "create" God.

The notion of a Primordial Man, which was later
to play an important role in the Kabbalah, makes its
first appearance in Jewish thought in the literature of
Merkaveh mysticism. A work entitled *Shi'ur Koma*
(The Measure of [the Divine] Body), which dates from

> *The notion of a Primordial Man, which was later
> to play an important role in the Kabbalah, makes
> its first appearance in Jewish thought in the
> literature of* Merkaveh *mysticism.*

---

before the sixth century c.e., describes the ascent to the
celestial throne and the vision of a gigantic supernal
man imprinted with magical letters and names.

Scholem regards the *Merkaveh/Hekhalot* literature
as a Jewish form of gnosticism, parallel but not identical to the Christian (and other non-Jewish) Gnosticism
of the second century c.e. According to Scholem, in the
Merkaveh mystics we find "a Jewish variation on one of
the chief preoccupations of the second and third century gnostics and hermetics: the ascent of the soul from
earth, through the sphere of the hostile planet-angels
and rulers of the cosmos, and its return to its divine
home in the 'fullness' of God's light, a return which, to
the gnostics' mind, signified redemption." The earliest
kabbalistic texts sought to establish a foundation in this
older "Jewish gnosticism," borrowing many of its images and vocabulary, but grafting these upon a new

cosmological and theosophical point of view, derived
from Greek, particularly Neoplatonic, thought.

The influence of Greek philosophical thought is
evident in a pre-kabbalistic work, *Sefer Yetzirah* (The
Book of Formation), written in Palestine in the third to
sixth centuries c.e., and later the subject of numerous
commentaries by the Kabbalists themselves. It is here
that the doctrines of the *Sefirot* and the *Otiyot Yesod*
(the Foundational letters), which later become central
symbols of the Kabbalah, make their first appearance.
As will be detailed in later chapters, these doctrines
bear the stamp of the Platonic ideas. In *Yetzirah*,
the *Sefirot* are supersensible numbers or metaphysical principles from which the world is created. The
twenty-two *Otiyot Yesod* are conceptualized in similar
terms, as archetypes from which God formed the cosmos. Together the *Sefirot* and the letters form the

---

*The Kabbalah proper is most often said
to originate in the anonymously authored*
Sefer HaBahir, *which appeared in Provence
late in the twelfth century.*

"thirty-two paths of wisdom" from which the world
was "graved and hewed."

The Kabbalah proper is most often said to originate
in the anonymously authored *Sefer HaBahir*, which
appeared in Provence late in the twelfth century. The
Bahir is steeped in language mysticism and contains a
further qualitative elaboration of the *Sefirot* doctrine.
Here the *Sefirot* are described as "the highest crown,"
"Wisdom," "the quarry of the Torah," "the throne of

splendor," etc. In this work *Merkaveh* and Greek elements are woven together in an almost *ad hoc* manner, and such familiar kabbalistic themes as the cosmic tree, *coincidentia oppositorum*, and the identification of God with the "All" make their appearance.

The Kabbalah of the school of Isaac the Blind also dates from this period. Isaac the Blind is the first Kabbalist consistently to use the word "*Sefirot*" and to relate these cosmic archetypes to the biblical enumeration of God's traits in Chronicles 29:11, where reference is made to God's greatness, power, beauty, victory, majesty, and sovereignty. Each of these was eventually adopted (by at least some Kabbalists) in the ordering of the lowest seven *Sefirot*.

~

While the Kabbalah was first developing in France, another influential Jewish pietistic movement in Germany, the *Hasidai Ashkenaz*, developed mystical themes in a direction different than that of the Kabbalah. The most important figure in this movement, Eleazar of Worms (d. c. 1230) put forth a mystical theology in which the supreme *Kavod* ("Divine Glory") or *Shekhinah* ("Divine Presence") is a holy being issuing from God and which acts as a divine intermediary in directing the world. The Hasidai Ashkenaz developed a detailed demonology, placed an emphasis on magic, and preached divine immanence in all things. Their influence was short-lived, but is detectable in certain of the Kabbalists, particularly those of the *Iyyun* circle.

From Provence, the Kabbalah rapidly spread to Gerona and then Castille. Among the first Geronese

Kabbalists of the early thirteenth century were Azriel, Ezra ben Solomon, Jacob ben Sheshet, and Moses ben Nachman (Nachmanides). In Azriel of Gerona we find a developed philosophical conception of the *Sefirot*, according to which they are the finite manifestations or powers of *Ein-Sof*, the Infinite Godhead. For Azriel, the *Sefirot* are a necessary part of God's totality and perfection, and they provide God with finite power to complement his infinite divine power. They are "the force behind every existent being in the realm of plurality," and are one with *Ein-Sof*, in the sense that the flame, the sparks, and the aura are one with the fire. In Azriel we find a sophisticated doctrine of *coincidentia oppositorum*: the *Sefirot* and even *Ein-Sof* are regarded as the "union of everything and its oppposite."

Among the earlier Spanish Kabbalists, Joseph Gikatilla (1249–c.1325) of Castille and Moses de Leon (1240–1305) are the most significant. Gikatilla provided a detailed exposition of the *Sefirot*, connecting each with a biblical name of God. He further explored their metaphysical and ethical meaning through detailed exegesis of what he regarded to be hidden references to the *Sefirot* in scripture.

The Zohar, the *locus classicus* and, according to tradition, the most holy of kabbalistic works, was presumably "discovered" by Moses de Leon in 1286. De Leon attributed this work to the second-century rabbinic sage Shimon Bar Yohai, but many felt, as do most scholars today, that de Leon was its major author. The main section of the Zohar is composed as a commentary on the Five Books of Moses, and this and several other additions (e.g., *Tikkunei ha-Zohar*) contain theosophical discourses on such topics as the hidden and manifest nature of God; the processes of creation; the *Sefirot* (which the Zohar calls by an abundance of other names); the nature of good

---

The Zohar, the locus classicus *and, according to tradition, the most holy of kabbalistic works, was presumably "discovered" by Moses de Leon in 1286.*

---

and evil; the masculine and feminine aspects of the divine; the nature of death, sleep, and dreams; and the essence of the human soul. The Zohar is not a systematic treatise, and its ideas must be pieced together from fragments from its numerous sections. Many of the ideas of the Lurianic Kabbalah are dynamic developments of concepts and symbols that first appear in the Zohar.

~

Much of the later history of the Kabbalah involves commentary, explication, and elaboration upon various zoharic themes. However, in the sixteenth century, in the town of Safed in Palestine, there developed a revival of kabbalistic speculation that is unparalleled in the history of Jewish mysticism. First, Moses Cordovero (1522–1570), and later Isaac Luria (1534–1572) developed theosophical systems, which, though based in the Zohar, were highly original. Cordovero developed a standard ordering of the *Sefirot* and a sophisticated theory in which each of the *Sefirot* were said to be contained within each of the others. According to

Cordovero, each entity in the world obtains its identity through the relative admixture of sefirotic elements from which it is comprised. Further, since the *Sefirot* are created in the image of God's divine traits, individuals are enjoined to develop the sefirotic qualities within their own souls.

While Cordovero left numerous writings, Luria wrote comparatively little, and it is through the works of his disciples, most notably Chayyim Vital (1543–1620) that we are aware of Luria's unique system of thought, the most complex, insightful, and difficult version of kabbalistic theosophy.

Among Luria's original contributions to the Kabbalah are the doctrines of *Tzimtzum* (Divine contraction and concealment), *Shevirat ha-Kelim* (The Breaking of the Vessels), and *Tikkun ha-Olam* (The Repair and Restoration of the World). In contrast to prior Kabbalists who had put forth either a linguistic or

---

Luria held that the world was created through a negative act of divine concealment, contraction, and withdrawal.

"emanationist" view of creation, Luria held that the world was created through a negative act of divine concealment, contraction, and withdrawal. Originally God's infinite being is "all," and it is only through a divine contraction that a void is formed within which finite things can subsist. This void becomes the metaphysical "space" in which *Ein-Sof* emanates an infinity of worlds and beings, the first and most significant of which is the Primordial Man (*Adam Kadmon*).

According to Luria the *Sefirot* are emanated as "lights" from the ears, nose, mouth, and eyes of the Primordial Man. These lights emanate and return, leaving behind a residue from which the "vessel" for each *Sefirah* is formed. A second light projected from the eyes of *Adam Kadmon* fills these vessels, completing the formation of each of the ten *Sefirot: Keter* (Crown) or *Ratzon* (Will), *Chochmah* (Wisdom), *Binah* (Understanding), *Chesed* (Loving-kindness), *Gevurah* (Strength) or *Din* (Judgment), *Tiferet* (Beauty) or *Rachamim* (Compassion), *Netzach* (Glory), *Hod* (Splendor), *Yesod* (Foundation), and *Malchut* (Kingship). The *Sefirot*, which are also conceptualized as the crown, brains, torso, and limbs of the Primordial Man, are the ten archetypal elements of the world. They are organized into a series of five "Worlds" (the Worlds of Primordial Man, "Nearness," "Creation," "Formation," and "Making"), the lowest of which, *Assiyah* or Making, provides the substance of our earth.

According to Luria the sefirotic vessels are unable to contain the light that was meant to fill them, and a majority of them are shattered, with the remainder (the upper three *Sefirot*) being "displaced." The result of this "Breaking of the Vessels" is that exile and discord holds sway throughout the cosmos. Shards from the broken vessels fall through the metaphysical void, entrapping sparks of divine light in "evil husks" (the *Kellipot*) that form the basis of the *Sitra Achra*, "the Other Side," a realm of evil, darkness, and death. Chaos reaches throughout the cosmos, as the masculine and feminine aspects of the deity, the Celestial "Mother" and "Father," represented by the *Sefirot Chochmah* and *Binah*, turn their backs on one another, disrupting the flow of divine energy throughout all the worlds.

Luria held that the restoration and repair of the broken vessels is largely in the hands of humankind. In freeing the divine sparks from the *Kellipot* and restoring them to God, and reestablishing the flow of masculine and feminine divine energies, man acts as a partner in the creation and redemption of the world, and is actually said to complete God Himself. *Tikkun ha-Olam*, the Restoration of the World, involves the reorganization of the broken vessels into a series of *Partzufim*, "Visages" or personality structures of God. According to Scholem, the *Partzufim* actually represent the evolution of the Primordial Man (*Adam Kadmon*) as it evolves toward a restored and redeemed world.

Lurianic ideas were prominent in the seventeenth-century messianic movement surrounding Sabbatei Zevi in Poland. They are clearly articulated in the kabbalistic works of Moses Chayyim Luzzatto (1707–1747) and were also highly influential among the Hasidim, who interpreted the Kabbalah in philosophical and psychological terms. Such early Hasidim as Dov

---

Lurianic ideas were prominent in the seventeenth-century messianic movement surrounding SabbateiZevi in Poland.

Baer of Mezhirech, who assumed leadership of the Hasidic movement from its founder, Israel Baal Shem Tov, in 1760; Schneur Zalman of Lyady (1745–1813),

the first Lubavitcher rebbe; and his pupil Aharon Halevi
Horowitz of Staroselye (1766–1728); made important
contributions to and original elaborations upon the
Lurianic symbols.

From *Kabbalistic Metaphors: Jewish Mystical Themes in Ancient and Modern Thought.*

Sanford L. Drob is Director of Psychological Assessment and the Senior Forensic
Psychologist at Bellevue Hospital in New York. He holds doctorate degrees in Philosophy from Boston University and in Clinical Psychology from Long Island University. In
1987 he co-founded, and for several years served as editor-in-chief of, the *New York
Jewish Review*, a publication addressing the interface between traditional Judaism and
contemporary thought.

III
The Study
of Kabbalah

5

The Study of Origins
of the Kabbalah

Joseph Dan

One of the most perplexing problems facing the historian when analyzing texts, especially texts concerning the history of ideas, is: To what extent can one take into account documentation that does not exist? The methodological answer to this question is, of course, that one should not do so at all. Yet it is rare, if not completely impossible, that a writer of history does not rely intuitively on his expectations concerning future discoveries. Every time one uses a phrase like "following this evidence, we may assume," he actually means: "We do not have as yet enough evidence, but I am sure that in the future more material proving this will be discovered." This is a natural tendency that if not carried too far, enables the scholar to suggest parts

of a historical picture even when there is not sufficient
textual material to support it. As long as a clear distinction is made between extant proof and expectations of
future discoveries, this attitude is acceptable in very
moderate doses.

It is my thesis in this Introduction that the study of
the origins of the Kabbalah in the last seventy years was
based on highly exaggerated expectations concerning
future discoveries, and that old conclusions should
now be reevaluated and changed. Because these expectations have not materialized, holding on to them
in the present circumstances is counterproductive. A
new understanding of the basic phenomena of the
emergence of the Kabbalah in the Middle Ages should
be based on a more rigorous adherence to the material
we have, and should take into account the possibility

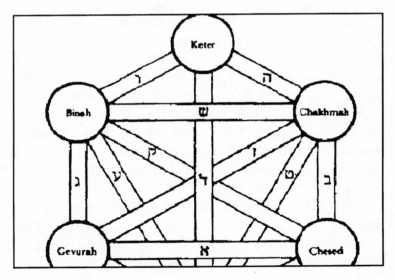

It is my thesis in this Introduction that the study of the origins of the Kabbalah in the last seventy years was based on highly exaggerated expectations concerning future discoveries, and that old conclusions should now be reevaluated and changed.

that what has not been discovered up to now does not exist.

A scholar surveying the situation of Jewish studies in the beginning of the twentieth century was, understandably, extremely hopeful concerning the possibility of dramatic future discoveries. Many of the major libraries of Hebrew books and manuscripts had not been catalogued. Hundreds of private collections were scattered around the world, untouched by scholars. Vast subjects were not mentioned in any scholarly publication. In that situation, to assume that something that had not yet been found did not exist was nearly impossible. It was evident to any clear-eyed observer that this was a scholarly discipline taking its first steps, and that many surprises and meaningful discoveries awaited in every corner. The discovery of the Cairo *Genizah* at the end of the nineteenth century gave a meaningful boost to the feeling that documents unlocking the secrets of the past were waiting for the scholar all over the world.

What may be said about Jewish studies in general may be said, with far more emphasis, concerning the study of Jewish mysticism. The amount of scholarly attention that this field received was meager, and most of the published works were never read by scholars. Whole schools and whole centuries of Jewish mysticism were completely unknown to scholarship. In these circumstances, the hope that the answer to every problem was waiting in the next manuscript, the next library catalogue, was well-founded.

It is understandable, therefore, that historical studies of Jewish intellectual, cultural, and religious ideas have been imbued with the feeling that whatever is unknown and unclear today will be known and documented tomorrow. It was possible to assume and postulate, on the basis that confirmation would be presented very soon, when the analysis of material in libraries and collections proceeded.

Concerning Jewish mysticism, this attitude was further encouraged by the intense and rapidly developing study of gnosticism. Nineteenth-century Jewish scholars repeatedly emphasized the similarity of the Kabbalah and gnostic mythological symbolism as known from the antignostic polemical works of the Church fathers. Writers who treated the Kabbalah with empathy, like Nachman Krochmal, joined writers who opposed the Kabbalah and saw it as a non-Jewish and anti-Jewish phenomenon, like Heinrich Graetz and Solomon Rubin, in postulating a connection, or even a dependence, between the kabbalistic ten *sefirot* and the gnostic pleroma. The field of gnosticism witnessed dramatic progress at that time, when new authentic gnostic sources were discovered, and new insights concerning the origins and nature of this heresy were discovered and analyzed. A belief that in the immediate future the whole complex of problems relating to the history of the early Kabbalah and its relationship to gnosticism would be clarified and documented seemed to be a most reasonable one. It seems to me, therefore, that the study of the Kabbalah in the first half of the present century can be characterized as being based on a mixture of texts and hopes; texts were appreciated for themselves, but also were seen as representing future discoveries. With this century nearing its end, we should, I believe, reexamine this attitude and see what can be retained and what must be discarded when the circumstances have completely changed.

From *Jewish Mysticism: The Middle Ages.*

Professor Joseph Dan is the Gershom Scholem Professor of Kabbalah at Hebrew University of Jerusalem. Born in Bratislava, Slovakia in 1935, he immigrated with his parents to Jerusalem in 1938. He received his B.A. (1956), M.A. (1958), and Ph.D. (1963) from Hebrew University. Professor Dan has served as the Head of the Institute for Jewish Studies in Hebrew University, and as the Director of the Jewish University and National Library. He has also served as a visiting professor at UCLA, UC Berkeley, Brown University, Colombia University, Harvard University, Princeton Institute of Advanced Study, and University College, London. Professor Dan has published over forty books in Hebrew and English. He was the recipient of the 1997 Israel Prize.

6

The Problems with Teaching Kabbalah

Eliahu Klein

Whenever I teach Kabbalah or Jewish mysticism, I always preface the course or lecture with the question: What do you want to get out of Kabbalah? The answers range from "I'm looking for a spiritual path (as long as I don't have to commit to anything!)" to "Kabbalah will make me wealthy," "Kabbalah will make me sexy," "Kabbalah will make me powerful," and "I'm wondering what I'm missing in Judaism." It is very rare to hear someone say, "I wish to transform my life and Kabbalah will help me," or, "I would like to study Kabbalah so that I can get close to God."

The Kabbalah of Luria and his school is a path utilizing a complex system to transform a tradition that has gone through enormous changes in the past 3,000

years (and in some areas has never changed). On one
side, Lurianic meditations are the most imaginative and
complex contemplations ever devised in the history of
Judaism. These meditations clearly guide the practitioner toward a complete transformation on all levels of
consciousness until one can attain a *unio mystica* —
a mystical union with God. On the other hand, the
Lurianic tradition contains some of the most stringent
and austere practices of Judaism. This is the great
paradox of Kabbalah. It is the path of complete transformation, when one meditates on the mandalas (reality maps) of evolutionary cosmologies as they link up
with Jewish religious practices. And yet it contains
some of the most reactionary attitudes in the history of
Judaism, in relation to sin, penance, women, souls,
punishment, non-Jews, homosexuals, and intimacy.

The question is, why the disparity between the

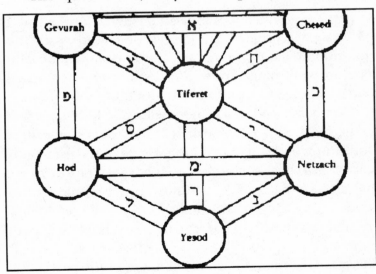

expansive consciousness of its meditations and cosmologies and the rigidity of attitude toward many
practices? I believe the following conclusions may be
controversial, but then, the publishing of this text is
controversial. Rabbis Isaac Luria and Haim Vital understood consciously or unconsciously that these teachings and meditation practices were very revolutionary
in their creation of an interdependency between the

---

*Lurianic meditations are the most imaginative and
complex contemplations ever devised in the history
of Judaism.*

---

highest and lowest realms in existence. These mystics
understood that by practicing these meditations and
through intense immersion into these teachings, one
could easily transcend the mundane. A practitioner
could attain a dangerous realization that there was only
higher consciousness. One need only to meditate upon
God's Names and liberate oneself through the study of
these texts to the point that *no external practice* was
needed anymore. Jewish ritual law would disappear
into the cosmic realm of pure *sefirot* and the inward
manifestation of Cosmic Archetypes such as the Great
Countenance or the Great Mother, *Ima Ilaah*. There
would be nothing left of the essential anchors and
grounding factors of Jewish religious and communal
life. Thus, the founders of this school of Kabbalah
devised and included within their system a comprehensive series of austerities and mental and emotional
attitudes that would maintain the existing system of

Torah traditions so that traditional Jewish continuity
would be in place.

History proved the worst-case scenario in the Sab-
batean adventure and the following Frankist disaster.
Shabbtai Tzvi (in the seventeenth century) not only
saw himself as the fulfillment of the law, but converted
to Islam (when the other option was to be beheaded by
the Caliph of Istanbul); Jacob Frank used the sacred
idea of Lurianic Kabbalah, "the redeeming of the
trapped sparks from the depths," as an excuse to en-
courage his disciples to commit incest, adultery, and
finally convert en masse to Christianity, while convinc-
ing Polish Catholic authorities of Kaminiezc (in the
early eighteenth century) to burn and destroy thousands upon thousands of volumes of talmudic tracts, all
in the name of redeeming the sparks from the depths.

We see how sacred teaching can be used for ulte-
rior motives in the worst way. However, I have not seen
these motives in the current generation of students.
This is a generation of countless sincere seekers rooted,
on one side, in the great prosperity of America of the
past fifty years and, on the other side, still linked, for
good reason, to the great anger and despair of the
Holocaust generation (which I believe is imbedded
within the collective consciousness of world Jewry).
Finally, there is within a majority of Jews a sense of
connectedness to Judaism solely due to the existence
of the political and national entity of the State of Israel.
Now, while it is wonderful that so many millions of
Jews have a reason to remain Jewish, this is not strong
enough to assuage the confusion and inner questioning

of many Jewish seekers, regarding profound spiritual
questions that this postmodernist generation raises.
Knowing that there is affluence in their lives, knowing
that there is a State of Israel (*Medinat Yisrael*) did not
stop literally hundreds of thousands *highly educated
and affluent* secular Buddhists, Sufic Muslims, reborn
Christians, and New Age yogis and yoginis. It is the
profound worldview and transformational meditation
practices of Kabbalah that have the power and wisdom
capacity to imbue Jewish practitioners and friends with
a meaningful understanding of life and to nurture the
unfolding of the soul—practices rooted in Judaism
itself. I don't limit the answer to Kabbalah; I include
chasidic methods, such as the direct path to God of the
Baal Shem Tov, the personal talking to God method of
Rabbi Nachman's school, the Habad way of theosophical contemplation, and the positivist radical determin-
ism of the Ishbitzer-Radziner School. Finally, I must
mention the spiritual path in which I was raised and
nurtured: the Lithuanian path of self-work, otherwise
known as the *Mussar* movement. These are some of
the ways and methods that can benefit Jewish seekers
in a profound and meaningful way. Every and any
tradition in Judaism that enables and empowers Jewish
seekers to deepen their understanding and practice of
Judaism ought to be welcomed, appreciated, and hon-
ored. The Kabbalah of the Ari (Rabbi Yitzchak Luria-
Ashkenazi and his Lion Cubs) is one such tradition.

The premise of this work is not just a historical,
analytical, or legendary focus; for those, there are many
studies by academic writers and historians such as

Dubnow, Scholem, or Idel. For the ethical teachings of this period there is the exemplary work of Professor Lawrence Fine in his book *Safed Spirituality* (Paulist Press). Nevertheless, I do part with academic methodology in two areas.

1. The most important emphasis of Lurianic Kabbalah is its spiritual significance and its potential power to transform the students and seekers who immersed themselves in these traditions.

2. There is a real possibility of applying these teachings in our personal lives. To look at the following mystical text as a guide and reality map, here are some issues that we need to raise. Are we studying Kabbalah because we wish to be known as kabbalists or mystics? Or to get a degree in Jewish studies? Are we studying Kabbalah because we are bored and curious? Are we studying Kabbalah because of a recent article we perused in *Time* or *Newsweek* magazine?

---

*Will Kabbalah give me the practical
and theoretical tools to live a profoundly
meaningful life?*

It is hoped that we will ask the following questions: Is Kabbalah the path that will answer the profound spiritual questions that constantly vex me? Will Kabbalah give me the practical and theoretical tools to live a profoundly meaningful life? Will Kabbalah empower me to spiritually empower my loved ones? Will Kabbalah help me connect with God in a direct and real way?

From *Kabbalah of Creation: Isaac Luria's Earlier Mysticism.*

Eliahu Klein has taught Kabbalah and Hasidism for over twenty-five years throughout North America. He was raised in the orthodox rabbinical worlds of Telz and Lakewood *yeshivot* and apprenticed under some of the greatest Jewish spiritual teachers of this generation, including Rabbi Aryeh Kaplan, Rabbi Shlomo Twerski of Denver, and Rabbi Shlomo Carlebach. Eliahu Klein received a private *smichah* (rabbinic ordination) from the late Rabbi Aryeh Kaplan three months before his untimely death in 1983.

7

Studying the Kabbalah

Noson Gurary

The teachings of Chasidism create the possibility for every person, including one who does not possess a lofty soul, and who has not purified himself, to be able to grasp and comprehend Godliness. By explaining the ideas of the esoteric part of the Torah, and making them accessible to the intellect, Chasidism enables everyone to comprehend even this part of Torah. Moreover, not only can he grasp this with the intelligence of the divine soul that resides within him, but also with the intelligence of the intellectual soul, and even with the intelligence of the animal soul.

There are four dimensions or levels of meaning and interpretation in the Torah: *Peshat*, the "plain meaning" of the text; *remez*, "allusion," in which a deeper meaning is hinted at but not stated explicitly;

derush, the homiletical and ethical explanation of the Torah; and *sod*, the esoteric dimension.

It must be noted that these four dimensions or levels of meaning in the Torah are four aspects of the same Torah and are inseparable from one another. The *Zohar* refers to the esoteric teachings of the Torah as "the soul of the Torah," and its exoteric teachings as "the body of the Torah." Just as the body without a soul is cold and dead, so, too, say the kabbalists, is Torah-study that is not vitalized by pondering its inner dimensions. Of course, the reverse also applies — study of the esoteric aspects of the Torah without the performance of the commandments makes such study "like a soul without a body — aimlessly floating about in a void." (The importance of the performance of the practical commandments in the chasidic world view, and the

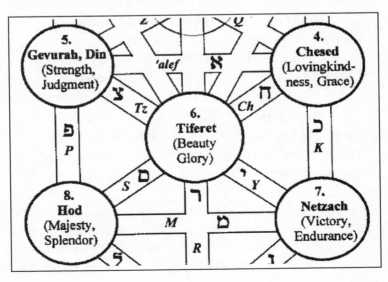

*Just as the body without a soul is cold and dead,
so, too, say the kabbalists, is Torah-study that is
not vitalized by pondering its inner dimensions.*

danger of antinomianism will be discussed later at
length).

Nevertheless, the Talmud and major codifiers, including Maimonides and R. Moshe Isserles (the *Ra-
mah*), rule that there are a number of preconditions
and limitations proscribing learning and teaching Kabbalah. One of the later authorities of Jewish law cites
several opinions that "one should not learn Kabbalah . . . until the age of forty . . . particularly
since sanctity, purity, alacrity, and an untainted soul are
required for this." Even those who fulfilled these conditions were taught the principles of Kabbalah in the
most discreet way, without making the matter public.
Moreover, kabbalistic texts themselves endorse these
restrictions, as we see from the words of the *Zohar*:
"One may not reveal the secrets of the Torah other than
to a person who is wise and has studied Scripture and
Talmud, whose studies endure, and who is God-fearing
and learned in everything." R. Shimon bar Yochai, the
author of the *Zohar*, confirms that he was given permission to reveal the mysteries of the Torah to his
colleagues only. R. Shimon and his circle of disciples,
known as the *chevraya kadisha* ("the holy fellowship"), are the classic representation of those whose
entire occupation is Torah study.

Similarly, R. Chaim Vital, the chief disciple and

codifier of the *Arizal*—R. Yitzchak Luria, the famed
sixteenth-century kabbalist of Safed, Israel—writes that

> Man must study the wisdom of the Kab-
> balah, but first, his body must be purified. This
> is brought about by fulfilling the *mitzvahs* [the
> commandments], which serve this purpose and
> are essential thereto. Only after this can the soul
> radiate in this body like a candle within a
> lantern—shining and invigorating him through
> understanding the secrets of the Torah, and
> revealing its depths.

Several reasons are given for these restrictions.
Among them: Discussing these very subtle matters in
public is disrespectful toward God, as the verse states,
"It is the glory of God to conceal a thing" (Proverbs
25:2); it is impossible for a created being (excluding
those who have reached an elevated spiritual level) to
understand these matters clearly; as a result of uninten-
tional misunderstanding, one might perceive a separation in that which is absolutely unified; and so on.

Nevertheless, R. Yitzchak Luria stated that "in
these latter generations, it is permitted and is also
a *mitzvah* to reveal this wisdom [the esoteric teachings of Kabbalah]." In the words of another distinguished kabbalist:

> The decree against open involvement with
> the True Wisdom [i.e., Kabbalah] was for a
> limited period of time, namely, up until the year
> 1490. From then onwards, the decree was an-

nulled and it is permissible to occupy oneself with the study of the *Zohar*. Since the year 1540, it is a most commendable precept to be occupied with this study in public, for both the great and the ordinary person. It is by virtue of this merit, and no other, that the King Messiah will come in the future. It is therefore improper to be lazy in this matter.

Nevertheless, even during the time of the *Arizal*, the revelation of this knowledge was not widespread. It was only with the advent of the Ba'al Shem Tov, and through his efforts, that the extensive and all-embracing dissemination of this wisdom began. This was in accordance with the response he received from the Messiah to disseminate these teachings (as explained earlier).

However, it was especially after the revelation of the intellectual branch of Chasidism, the *Chabad*-Lubavitch dynasty, that these teachings were revealed in a way that can "sustain and nourish," for then Chasidism was articulated in terms of man's intellectual understanding and in rational language, which is called "food" for the soul. This was particularly so after the imprisonment and subsequent release of Rabbi Shneur Zalman — "after Petersburg," as mentioned earlier. (The reason for the revelation of the esoteric teachings and the license to study and propagate them specifically in the latter generations was discussed more fully in the previous chapter).

〜

What is the methodology of Chasidism that enables it to reveal the ideas of the esoteric part of the Torah, "and make them accessible to the intelligence of the intellectual soul, and even to the intelligence of the animal soul," so that even ordinary people who do not possess lofty souls and have not purified themselves "will be able to make unifications and ascents of soul" just like the greatest saints?

Rabbi Shalom Dov-Ber of Lubavitch (1860–1920), the fifth Lubavitcher Rebbe, explains that although the content and subject matter of chasidic meditation is primarily the kabbalistic writings of the *Arizal*, nevertheless, the methodology of their study is very different from the traditional methods of speculative Kabbalah. The basis of *Kabbalah* is the verse in Ezekiel's vision of the Divine Chariot—"Upon the Throne was the appearance of the likeness of Man" (Ezekiel 1:21). In the writings of the *Arizal*, Godliness has thus been "clothed" in "the likeness of man," that is, abstract divine matters are made accessible to human under-

---

The basis of Kabbalah is the verse in Ezekiel's vision of the Divine Chariot— "Upon the Throne was the appearance of the likeness of Man" (Ezekiel 1:21).

---

standing by depicting them in human terms and images, allowing the mind to grasp what is essentially beyond human comprehension. The writings of the *Arizal* are indeed replete with anthropomorphic terminology and imagery. For example: The *sefirah* ("divine emanation") of *chochmah* ("wisdom") is referred to as *abba* ("father"). The *sefirah of binah* is referred to as *imah* ("mother"). The interaction of these two *sefirot* is known as *zivug* ("coupling" or "union"). The products of this union are *ben* ("son", referring to the configuration of six *sefirot*, from *chesed* to *yesod*) and *bat* ("daughter", the *sefirah* of *malchut*), and so on. Of course, these terms should not be taken at face value. The intention is only to understand Godliness by way of human metaphors, as the Sages of the Talmud noted: "The Torah speaks in the language of man," in order to make abstract concepts comprehensible to the human mind. Nevertheless, divine emanations are depicted in human terms.

The methodology of Chasidism, however, is exactly the opposite. Chasidic philosophy is based on the verse, "We shall make man in Our image" (Genesis 1:26). Since man is the reflection of the divine realm, proper scrutiny of the human realm leads to understanding of the divine realm. Moreover, the human realm is easily accessible to all, and understanding of it does not require a special level of sanctity and lengthy preparations and purifications. After proper introspection, by stripping the soul's qualities of their human connotations, one may have a clear view of the divine realm. By understanding the operation of the faculties of one's own soul—such as *chochmah*, *binah*, and *da'at*—one can come to an understanding of *chochmah*, *binah*, and *da'at* above. Chasidism thus uses the method of abstraction rather than anthropomorphism. Put somewhat differently, *Kabbalah* defines (and thus delimits) Godliness, by "clothing Godliness within a human form." Chasidism, by contrast, endeavors to strip away the corporeal and human aspects of the faculties of one's soul, and in this way come to an understanding of abstract and unformed Godliness, as the verse states, "From my flesh I see God" (Job 19:26). Consequently, it is possible to apprehend far loftier levels of Godliness—those levels that cannot be clothed in human terms—than can be understood through traditional *Kabbalah*. Moreover, this process of teaching oneself to see Godliness through the soul's faculties has the effect of making these faculties themselves Godly. (Note that this recalls the previous definition of the contribution and innovation of Chasidism—that it changes the nature of one's character, making it Godly).

From *Chasidism: Its Development, Theology, and Practice.*

Noson Gurary is an ordained rabbi and Jewish judge. He received his rabbinical ordination at the United Lubavitcher Yeshiva in Brooklyn, New York. He recently received his doctorate in Jewish philosophy from the Moscow Lomonosov University in Russia. Rabbi Gurary is currently the executive director of the *Chabad* Houses in upstate New York and has taught in the Judaic Studies Department at State University of New York, Buffalo, for many years.

IV
Who Is
a Kabbalist?

8

The Kabbalist

Zalman Meshullam Schachter-Shalomi

Kabbalist, mystic, and *ba'al m'qubal* all refer to one who has become adept in the secret lore, the Kabbalah. His studies centered on books like the Zohar and the writings of the Ari. His prayer was not the ordinary pronunciation of the words, but a secret code of permutations of holy names. Because of the kabbalist's belief that he served as a lamp lighter to bring about the effulgence of the Divine Spheres, the predominant view was that the kabbalist held the keys to bring about the influx from above. Who better than the kabbalist could bring about health, wealth, and progeny? Small wonder therefore that all kinds of practical powers were said to reside in him. If he managed to see "the light that illumined the world from end to end" and that "God reserved for the righteous," he could see and hear what others could not.

A rebbe's image depends on the reputation he has among the hometown esoterics. He is a great rebbe if he manages to impress and direct them. He will not do this by being kind and gentle with them. Instead, he wants to give them new light and revelation. The kabbalistic hasid wants his rebbe to be an open channel to the innermost part of the Torah. He wants access to ever new revelations. For the thirsting soul, the puzzle as to how the Infinite creates the finite, and how and why the Infinite is concerned for humanity, is never satisfactorily resolved. The way in which answers are newly wrung from eternal ineffability, expressed in the language of Torah, captured in the vessels of mitzvot, and experienced in meditation, is of utmost importance to such a hasid.

The speculative aspect of the Kabbalah, which gives access to the *mysterium fascinans* and leads the soul to the threshold of the *mysterium tremendum*, finds spokesmen and seekers in every age. In Hasidism,

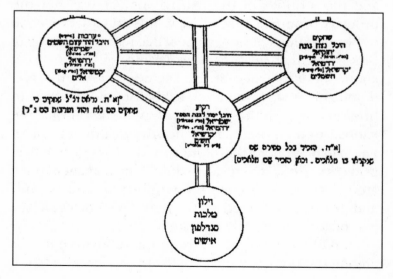

each great rebbe is seen as the repository of Kabbalah. Rebbes reveal to hasidim, both in the public lecture

---

In Hasidism, each great rebbe is seen as the repository of Kabbalah.

---

and in the privacy of the yehidut, the arcana that speak to their condition.

The key difference between the contribution of Hasidism and that of the Kabbalah was that these arcana became accessible to experience with the advent of the Besht. When R. Dovber, the Magid of Mezhirech, came to the Besht, the latter asked him if he had studied the Kabbalah. When R. Dovber replied in the affirmative, he was asked to interpret a particular passage in the Lurianic *Etz Hayim*. When the Magid had exhausted the academic exegesis, the Besht stood up and repeated the passage. This time the Magid actually saw the realities discussed in the passage. This is what made him into a disciple. What was merely an esoteric game of verbal arrangements had, in Hasidism, become a profound experience. The arena of Kabbalah now shifted from the theological to the psychological realm.

Habad continued this tradition. With R. Shneur Zalman, there began a new era of reconciliation of rationalism and the esoteric. Even the academic Kabbalah gained in the process. For those who wanted more of the imaginative, R. Nahman of Bratzlav became the master. R. Israel of Kozhinitz, R. Hirsch (Zvi) of Zyditchov, and R. Isaac of Komarno were the mentors

for those who wished to follow the path of the classical
Kabbalah.

From *Spiritual Intimacy: A Study of Counseling in Hasidism.*

Rabbi Zalman Schachter-Shalomi is the moving spirit behind ALEPH, Elat Chayyim, and
much of the current spiritual awakening in Judaism. He was ordained at the Lubavitcher
Yeshiva and received his doctorate from the Hebrew Union Institute. He has studied
with Sufi Masters, Buddhist teachers, Native American elders, Catholic monks, and
humanistic and transpersonal psychologists. He is the founder of the Spiritual Eldering
Institute, which sponsors workshops providing the psychological and spiritual tools for
people of all ages to grow into elderhood. He is the "Holder of the Chair of World
Wisdom" at Naropa Institute in Boulder, CO.

9

The Kabbalah of the Ari

Adin Steinsaltz

The book that first made known the personality and life of Ha-Ari (The Lion) was written only a short time after his death. Called *Shiv-chei Ha-Ari* (*Praises of the Ari*), it attempted to relate whatever was known of the life of the Ari—as Isaac Luria was called—and to enhance the memory of him with stories of divination and miracles. Much was afterwards told and retold of his visions and revelations and of his ability to see the depths of the souls of his disciples—of Elijah the Prophet, who used to appear before him—of his power to cast out *dybuks* (demons), and other works of wonder that he performed. But the greatest wonder and the supreme miracle of the Ari is not in any of the marvels with which he may have impressed certain of his disciples—it is the historical fact of his achievement.

In the year 1570, a virtually unknown man came from Egypt to the city of Safed in upper Galilee. He lived in Safed only two years; he hardly wrote anything at all and merely taught a small group of disciples. At the end of these two years he died, being no more than thirty-eight years of age. But through the teachings of these two short years, the Ari, or Isaac ben Shlomo Luria, created an entirely new world. Our Divine Rabbi Yitzchak, as he has been called ever since, created a new system that in many ways changed Judaism, theoretically and historically. He is numbered among those few singular personalities who, by themselves, created an epoch, and without whose achievement it is impossible to understand the history of the years after them. What is incredible is the extremely short period of time in which this work was accomplished.

When the Ari came to Safed, he found an enchanting little city, a city almost as fascinating as himself. For some quite inexplicable reason, this obscure place in

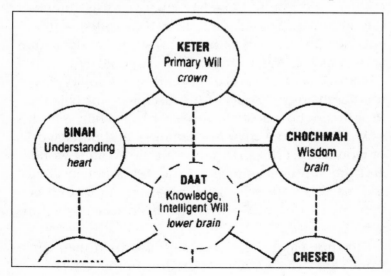

upper Galilee, which was even then older than re-
corded memory, had become in the sixteenth century
the spiritual capital of the whole Jewish people. Some
of the greatest Jewish minds of the age had begun to
gather there, drawn from among those who had been
forced out of Spain and other European countries as
well as from the East. For several decades during the

---

*Our Divine Rabbi Yitzchak, as he has been
called ever since, created a new system that
in many ways changed Judaism, theoretically
and historically.*

---

middle of the sixteenth century, so many learned scholars lived in Safed that the last bold attempt was made at
that time to renew the institution of the Sanhedrin and
establish a high court and governing body for the Jews
of the world.

Among the outstanding figures gathered there were
great codifiers of the Law, like Joseph Karo, author of
the famous *Shulchan Aruch*; the last of the great poets
of Spanish culture, like Shlomo Alkevitz, composer of
the Sabbath hymn, *"Lechah Dodi"*; and Israel Najara,
the poet. Also living in Safed were some of the writers
of the profoundly moving books on moral action,
works that had such a lasting influence on the people.
Finally, there were the great kabbalists of the time,
chief among them, Moses Cordovero.

The city was remarkable, however, not only because of the great men who lived in it, but also for the
general atmosphere, which included all the inhabit-
ants. It was a sort of dream city-state, a realization of

certain spiritual ideals, almost Messianic, to which the
people of Israel had always aspired. What characterized it was the extreme spiritual tension in which the
whole city was absorbed. Artisans and merchants,
scholars and converts just returning to Judaism, and
people of all ages and backgrounds were devoted to
studying the Torah and practicing the Torah. The city
was full of synagogues, schools, and houses of study, all
of them permeated with the belief that it was possible
to bring all Jews to his level of responsiveness, and that
the final redemption was imminent.

Just when this city was at the height of its spiritual
flowering, Isaac Luria came and conquered it with his
personality and gave it his teaching, which spread with
amazing rapidity from this city — then the very center
of Jewry — to all the scattered Jewish communities of
the world, so that in a few years, there was hardly a
single community, from Yemen to Russia, from Iraq to
Germany, that had not been dazzled by the revelations
of the Ari and did not accept them as the fulfillment of
Jewish thought.

~

The Spanish expulsion had been a historic turning
point not only politically and practically but also intellectually and spiritually. Besides being uprooted from a
land where Jews had lived for a thousand years, countless Jews had failed to stand the test and had converted.
These converts were merely a handful of renegades;
they included people from the finest and most aristo-
crat families, those imbued with Jewish culture as well
as a broad general culture. The disappointment of the

Jewish community in the converts caused the Spanish émigrés to reexamine their relation to culture, in particular to religious philosophy. It appeared that the magnificent intellectual structure of their Judaized Aristotelian philosophy could not support them in times of trial. Thus, the old controversy about a satisfactory

---

Within a generation or two after the expulsion from Spain, it was acceded that the Kabbalah was the closest thing to a theology that Judaism had.

---

system of thought that would also provide an inner incentive for the life of Jewish piety and *mitzvot* was finally decided: the true values and ideas of the Jewish people should not be sought in systems foreign to it, but in its own esoteric teachings—the Kabbalah. In fact, within a generation or two after the expulsion from Spain, it was acceded that the Kabbalah was the closest thing to a theology that Judaism had.

The teachings of the Kabbalah go back to antiquity. It is said that even the "sons of the prophets" of the period of the First Temple developed certain mystical concepts that became the beginning of the Kabbalah. In any case, by the time of the Second Temple, we find many indications of systems of esoteric lore, such as *Ma'aseh Breshit* (*Concerning Genesis*) and *Ma'aseh Merkavah* (*Concerning the Chariot*), which were passed on orally, from one generation of wise men to the next. In time, Kabbalah (that which is received) gradually revealed more of itself; basic books were written and circulated, and outstanding figures at vari-

ous times in history hinted at their relation to the
Kabbalah and at the way in which they drew from it.

In the fourteenth century, the Zohar was discovered in Spain, and this book became the basic kabbalistic text. Although not at all organized in any
systematic way, the Zohar still has a fairly clear system
of its own, and much of the work of later generations
has been nothing more than clarification, expansion,
and development of the system. Altogether, the literature of the Kabbalah is vast, including thousands of
books, but the fundamentals, to a degree, can be summarized briefly.

According to the Kabbalah, God acts on the world
and reveals himself through ten aspects, or emanations, called the *Ten Sefirot*. These *sefirot* are the
instruments through which the Divine fullness is revealed, God Himself being finite and devoid of all limits
and attributes in the world. The mutual relationship
between these *sefirot* and their various combinations
determine the essential manner and working of the
world, and especially of men. More particularly, the
people of Israel react to the union or separation or
constellation of the various *sefirot*, with all their power
for good and for ill. The evil in the world is derived
from a distortion of certain forces, and they can, in
turn, have a bad effect on the rest of creation. The
Torah, or Jewish scriptures is, on the whole, a revelation of the right way to behave so that the Divine plenty
will flow into the reality of the world. The carrying out
of the commandments (*mitzvot*) of the Torah acts in a
concrete way to make the *sefirot* combine properly to
cause this plenty to flow, while the transgression of the

commandments is an act of absolute evil that adds strength to the forces of wickedness and pollution in the world. The esoteric teaching, the Kabbalah, is the inner part of the Torah that explains the metaphysical

---

According to the Kabbalah, God acts on the world and reveals himself through ten aspects, or emanations, called the Ten Sefirot.

---

significance of every single movement and thought, and ultimately of the whole essence of the world. The man who attains genuine knowledge of the wisdom of the Kabbalah can, in certain respects, use the keys provided by this wisdom to reach a deeper and more complete closeness to God, and is able to change and "repair" the world in which he lives.

~

When the Ari came to Safed, he found the greatest systematizer of the Kabbalah, Moses Cordovero, still living there. Although the work of Kabbalah scholarship was at its height, the Ari had no new way of arranging the material, nor was there a new philosophic system to explain the Kabbalah. Modestly, he explained to his pupils that what he had acquired was the result of a long and wearying inner struggle and told of the joy of "doing" the *mitzvot*. Indeed, that which made him stand out was a new illumination, an independent and mystical revelation, and a new understanding of the Torah and the Kabbalah.

The system of thought propounded by the Ari did not merely add something to existing knowledge; it was an approach that, in its own way, encompassed and included previous forms of studying Torah and Kabbalah and provided a new interpretation. Thus, whole new fields of inquiry were opened up by the Kabbalah of the Ari. Its influence was so pervasive, it can be compared to the influence of the theory of relativity on modern physics.

The most thorough review of the Ari's revelation was set down in writing by his disciple, Chaim Vital. His book *Etz Chaim* (*Tree of Life*) contains thousands of the Ari's discoveries and interpretations, all written in the extremely concise and concentrated form of symbols traditional to kabbalistic rendering and with the addition of new symbolic methods. One of the most daring of his concepts was a new understanding of Creation, according to which the world was created

---

One of the most daring of his concepts was a new understanding of Creation, according to which the world was created by an act of Divine contraction.

---

by an act of Divine contraction. The infinite Divine light hid itself (contracted), and in the place that was formed by the absence of the light, there came into existence the place for the finite world. The world is therefore a reality drawing sustenance from the absence of a real being, and this nonbeing is derived from the infinite Divine power. The world is therefore encompassed and surrounded by the infinite essence of Divinity, while it, itself, consists of another kind of emanation of Divinity, in which the hidden and the revealed are intermingled. The Ari's system was in a sense a new theological approach in Judaism, emphasizing the somewhat pantheistic views of the Kabbalah, by which the world is seen to be included in the Divine but is not identical to Divinity. This system also provided a new interpretation to the meaning of evil, for at a certain stage in its coming into being, the world had to pass through a cataclysmic experience, "the breaking of the vessels." In other words, the *sefirot*, at an early phase of manifestation, did not fit together and were consequently shattered, and in their breaking up (the world of chaos), our world was created.

The world as we know it is a new combination and structure, made up of the contradictions and incompleteness resulting from the breaking of the vessels. The fragments of the higher world that was shattered, the "sparks" from the Divine light, are scattered throughout existence, some of them becoming part of the chain of Divine sovereignty in the world, or "chariot," and others falling out and becoming distorted, changing their form, and becoming the material world and even the forces of evil. Thus, it is the task of man to redeem these shattered fragments, or sparks, to find in them their higher significance, and to restore them to their Divine origin.

In fact, the entire course of life on earth toward its final redemption is the constant struggle to redeem the light that is hidden in the darkness, and when this process is completed, there will be revealed the true, whole structure. This is the meaning of the coming of the Messiah. Thus, according to this approach, the redemption of the sparks is the work of every Jew, and this work—which is done by keeping the Torah and

doing the *mitzvot,* by ascetic self-discipline and moral
restitution, by right intention in all one's deeds and
mystical unity—this work is the decisive factor in
redemption. Waiting for salvation is, therefore, not a
passive state of being; it is rather the active doing of
every person whose every thought and deed can con-
tribute to the redemption of the universe. This is at
least part of the reason for the enormous influence of
the Ari's teachings on the daily life of Jews in subsequent generations. The entire people became active
participants in the struggle for the "end of days."

It did not take long for the Ari's Kabbalah to become the Kabbalah, and everything that developed
after that, like the Chasidic movement, grew out of it.

It did not take long for the Ari's Kabbalah to
become the Kabbalah, and everything that
developed after that, like the Chasidic movement,
grew out of it.

His teachings were adopted by the common people —
not only by the great minds who made a study of
Kabbalah; it became the basis for a whole mystic literature and a broad moralist movement, and hundreds of
new customs and prayers were inspired by it. Inevita-
bly, it caused a change in perspective in the relations of
man, and the world, the Torah, and the Kabbalah.

What of the Ari himself? He left us in writing no
more than a few mystical poems, which are sung to this
day with a certain awe on the Sabbath, and several
Talmudic exegeses. Still, one can catch more than a
glimpse of the man between the lines of what he wrote

and in the disjointed descriptions of him by his disciples. A clear-eyed, saintly figure, whose look penetrated the unknown and who was, at the same time, extremely simple and straightforward in the small actions of daily life, seeing in them a great light. Together with this immense authority that he exercised was his profound humility, so natural to one for whom everything was open and manifest, so that he never seemed to have occasion to think about himself or his task in the same way that he used to tell about his visions and thoughts. Like a Moses, he stands at a crossroads in the history of the people, holding in his hand the key to the way through which the generations pass.

From *The Strife of the Spirit.*

Rabbi Adin Steinsaltz, scholar, teacher, mystic, scientist, and social critic, is internationally regarded as one of the leading rabbis in this century. The author of many books, he is best known for his monumental translation of and commentary on the Talmud. In 1988, Rabbi Steinsaltz was awarded the Israel Prize, his country's highest honor. He and his family live in Jerusalem.

V
Kabbalistic Texts

10

The Bahir: The Primary Text of Kabbalah

Aryeh Kaplan

Although the Bahir is the primary text of Kabbalah, it does not use this term, preferring the Mishnaic term, *Maaseh Merkavah,* which literally means "Workings of the Chariot," in allusion to Ezekiel's vision. It states that delving into these mysteries is as acceptable as prayer, but warns that it is impossible to do so without falling into error,

The Talmud states that the Kabbalah should be taught only through hints and allusions, and this is the course followed by the author of the Bahir. One who merely reads it as a book will find that large portions make little if any sense. It is not a subject for casual perusing, but for serious and concentrated study, and it was accepted among Kabbalists that the major texts were written so that they could be understood only when analyzed as an integrated whole. We are warned that one who reads the Kabbalah literally and shallowly is almost certain to misunderstand it.

The proper way to study any kabbalistic text is to take it as a whole, using every part to explain every other one. The student must find threads of ideas running through the text, and follow them back and forth, until the full meaning is ascertained. In a small text like the Bahir, this is relatively straightforward, and our index should be helpful. In larger texts such as the Zohar, this methodology assumes even greater importance, and without it, much of the writings of the Ari will appear like little more than gibberish.

One of the most important concepts revealed in the Bahir is that of the Ten Sefirot, and with the exception of three, their names are also introduced. Careful analy-

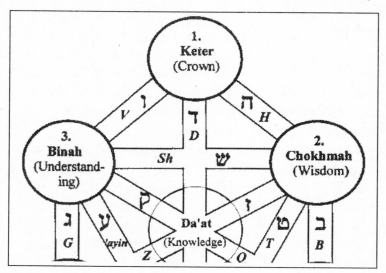

sis of these discussion yields much of what will be found in later kabbalistic works, as well as their rela-

---

The proper way to study any kabbalistic text is to take it as a whole, using every part to explain every other one. The student must find threads of ideas running through the text, and follow them back and forth, until the full meaning is ascertained.

---

tion to anthropomorphisms and the reason for commandments.

Particularly interesting is the order in which the Sefirot are given. The last seven of these correspond to the seven days of the week, and are derived from the verse *(1 Chronicles 29:11)*, "Yours O God are the Greatness, the Strength, the Beauty, the Victory and the Splendor, All (Foundation) that is in heaven and earth, Yours O God is the Kingdom." This is the order followed by most kabbalistic texts.

In the Bahir, however, the order of the last four is reversed. The last four Sefirot are then Kingship *(Aravot,* 7), Foundation (8), Victory (9), and Splendor (10). The reason given for this is that Kingship must be in the middle of the seven, and since it corresponds to the Sabbath, it is also fitting that it be the seventh Sefirah. Similarly, since Foundation corresponds to the sign of circumcision, it is fitting that it be eighth, since circumcision is performed on the eighth day.

With the exception of Beauty, Splendor and Kingship, all the Sefirot are given their standard names. Beauty is called the Throne of Glory, while Kingship is

called *Aravot*. Splendor is simply called the second
Victory. In a number of places, Foundation is also
called the Righteous One, the Life of Worlds, and "All".

~

Another important concept that is revealed is that
of reincarnation or *Gilgul*. It is interesting to note that
this idea is first introduced in the name of Rabbi Akiba.
This concept is used to explain the problem of apparent injustice and why even innocent children suffer
and are born maimed. The fact that Saadiz Gaon rejects
reincarnation is simple proof that he did not have
access to the secret teachings of the Kabbalah. This
concept is further developed in the Zohar, and in even
greater detail in the *Sefer Gilgulim* and other writings
of the Ari's school.

Other subjects included in the Bahir include an
interpretation of the letters of the Hebrew alphabet,
fifteen of which are mentioned. Such commandments
as *Tefillin, Tzitzit, Lulav*, and *Etrog,* as well as "sending
the mother bird" are discussed, usually in the context
of the Sefirot or other previously introduced concepts.
A number of ideas found in the *Sefer Yetzirah,* such as
the Thirty-two Paths of Wisdom, the twelve diagonal
boundaries, as well as the "Axis, Sphere and Heart" are
discussed. In general, numbers play a highly significant
role in the Bahir.

Two unusual terms are found in the Bahir, both of
which apparently refer to angels or angelic forces. One
is *Tzurah,* which literally means "form" while the
other is *Komah,* which can be translated as "structure."
In kabbalistic literature, these are more familiar in their

Aramaic form, the former being *Diukna,* and the latter, *Partzuf.* Other terms used for angels are Directors *(Manhigim)* and Functionaries *(Pekidim).*

Another important revelation is the various names of God. . . . The Name containing twelve letters, mentioned in the Talmud, is also discussed. This is also true of the Name consisting of seventy-two combinations, which is also derived. This name is mentioned in early Talmudic sources, and its derivation is discussed as early as 1100 by both Rashi (1040–1105) and the *Midrash Lekach Tov (Pesikta Zutrata).*

~

Tzimtzum

One of the important concepts introduced in the Bahir is that of Tzimtzum, the self-constriction of God's Light. This involves one of the most important philosophical concepts of the Kabbalah, as well as one which has been a source of confusion to many scholars.

The clearest statement of the Tzimtzum can be found in the writings of Rabbi Isaac Luria (1534–1572), known as the Ari, who headed the Safed school of Kabbalah. As described in *Etz Chaim* ("Tree of Life"), the process was as follows:

> Before all things were created . . . the Supernal Light was simple, and it filled all existence. There was no empty space. . . .
>
> When His simple Will decided to create all universes . . . He constricted the Light to the sides . . . leaving a vacated space. . . . This space was perfectly round. . . .

> After this constriction took place . . .
> there was a place in which all things could be
> created. . . . He then drew a single straight
> thread from the Infinite Light . . . and brought
> it into that vacated space. . . . It was through
> that line that the Infinite Light was brought
> down below. . . .

In its literal sense, the concept of Tzimtzum is
straightforward. God first "withdrew" His Light, forming a vacated space, in which all creation would take
place. In order for His creative power to be in that
space, He drew into it a "thread" of His Light. It was
through this "thread" that all creation took place.

Virtually all the later Kabbalists warn that the Tzimtzum is not to be taken literally, since it is impossible to
apply any spatial concept to God. Rather, this is speaking in a conceptual sense, since if God filled every

---

Virtually all the later Kabbalists warn that the
Tzimtzum is not to be taken literally, since it is
impossible to apply any spatial concept to God.

---

perfection, man would have no reason to exist. God
therefore constricted His infinite perfection, allowing a
"place" for man's free will and accomplishment.

Another important point stressed by many Kabbalists is the fact that the Tzimtzum did not take place in
God's essence, but in His Light. This Light was the first
thing brought into being, representing God's power of
creation, this itself having been brought into existence
for the purpose of creating the universe.

Many historians erroneously conclude that the Tzimtzum originated in the teachings of the Ari. Actually, however, it is a much older teaching, and a clear reference to it is found in the Zohar. Consider the following passage:

> At the head of the King's authority
> He carved out of the supernal luminescence
>   a Lamp of Darkness.
> And there emerged out of the Hidden of Hidden —
>   the Mystery of the Infinite —
>   an unformed line, imbedded in a ring . . .
>   measured with a thread. . . .

According to most Kabbalists, this is a direct reference to the Tzimtzum.

A close look in the Bahir will also reveal a clear allusion to the Tzimtzum. Rabbi Berachiah says that the Light was like a "beautiful object" for which the King had no place. It is explicitly stated that this light had existed earlier, but that there was no place in which to put it. Only after a "place" was provided could the light be revealed. The reference is clearly to the "thread" of Light mentioned in the *Etz Chaim,* which brought forth all creation. This is also the "unformed line embedded in a ring," mentioned in the Zohar.

The reason for the Tzimtzum stems from a basic paradox. God must be in the world, yet, if He does not restrict Himself from it, all creation would be overwhelmed by His Essence. Both the paradox and its resolution are clearly alluded to in the Bahir.

There is, however, a more difficult paradox in-

volved in the Tzimtzum. Since God removed His Light
from the vacated space, it must be empty of His Essence. Still, God must also fill this space, since "there is
no place empty of Him." This is a most basic paradox,
and it is closely related to the dichotomy of God's
imminence and transcendence.

The main point brought out by this paradox is the
fact that this space is only "dark" and "vacated" with
respect to us. The "Lamp of Darkness" mentioned in
the Zohar is "darkness" to us, but with relation to God,
it too is a "lamp." With respect to God, it is actually
light, since for Him it is as if the Tzimtzum never took
place. The reason for the Tzimtzum was so that creation could take place, and this is required for us, but
not for God. Close study indicates that this is precisely
the question and answer found in the opening statement of the Bahir.

It is particularly interesting to note that it is precisely with this apparent paradox that Rabbi Nehuniah
opens the Bahir. The main point of the theoretical
Kabbalah is to resolve the paradox of how an absolutely transcendental God can interact with His creation. The structure of the Sefirot and similar concepts

*The main point of the theoretical Kabbalah is to
resolve the paradox of how an absolutely
transcendental God can interact with His creation.*

are what form the bridge between God and the universe. Lest it be thought that this implies any change in
God Himself, Rabbi Nehuniah clearly states that the
darkness of the vacated space is actually light with

respect to God. The creation of the vacated space, as well as all worlds, spiritual and physical, that exist in it, did not in any way change or diminish God's Light.

Such an introduction is reminiscent of a similar warning found at the beginning of the *Idra Rabba,* one of the most mysterious portions of the Zohar, and one containing much anthropomorphic symbolism. At the very beginning of this section, Rabbi Shimon quotes the verse *(Deuteronomy 26:15),* "Cursed is the man who makes any image . . . and puts it in a hidden place." In the context in which it is used here, the "hidden place" refers to the highest supernal universes. Even though anthropomorphisms may be used in describing the Sefirot and other kabbalistic concepts, they are in no way meant to be taken literally.

Rabbi Nehuniah is giving a very similar warning at the beginning of the Bahir. Do not think that the Sefirot are lights coming to fill any darkness with respect to God, since for Him all is Light. In order to avoid error, Rabbi Nehuniah's name appears here without disguise — this principle is so important that it must be backed by the full prestige of the master himself.

From *The Bahir.*

Rabbi Aryeh Kaplan was born in New York City and was educated in the Torah Voda'as and Mir Yeshivot in Brooklyn. After years of study at Jerusalem's Mir Yeshiva, he was ordained by some of Israel's foremost rabbinic authorities. He also earned a master's degree in physics and was listed in *Who's Who in Physics in the United States.* In the course of a writing career spanning only twelve years, Rabbi Kaplan earned a reputation as one of the most effective, persuasive, scholarly, and prolific exponents of Judaism in the English language. He died on January 28, 1983, at the age of 48.

11

The Basic Concepts of Sefir Yetzirah

Leonard R. Glotzer

Sefer Yetzirah is a book of numbers and letters. The world was created with ten numbers and twenty-two letters. The numbers are associated with the ten emanations of God's light, known as *Sefirot*. The letters represent basic forces of nature. They are derived from flows of light between the *Sefirot*.

If all this sounds quite mystical and obscure, it is only because in reality it is. The concepts of Kabbalah are couched in everyday physical terms like light and flows, but they refer to spiritual ideas of a completely different nature. There is a parallelism, though, between the worlds. The physical world, being a result of the higher spiritual spheres, retains much of their structure. Thus, for example, the ten emanations are said to

manifest in the physical world as actual spheres surrounding the earth.

The creation of the world began by God emanating
the *Sefirot* (plural of *Sefirah*). They are known also as
"God's attributes." They are spiritual entities and are
not at all physical. Their exact nature has been a matter
of much kabbalistic debate.

In the *Zohar*, the positions the ten *Sefirot* assume
in relation to each other are described in at least three
seemingly incompatible ways.

1. *Each* Sefirah *is directly above the next*. God
   emanated the first *Sefirah*, and the first emanated the second, and so forth. This setup implies that the first *Sefirah* is closest to the source
   (God) and is thus holier than the second. The

מ"ד וכיון שצפה אברהם אבינו ע"ה והביט
וראה וחקר והבין וחקק וחצב וצרף וצר
ועלתה בידו אז נגלה עליו אדון הכל ב"ה
והושיבהו בחיקו ונשקו על ראשו וקראו
אוהבי וכרת לו ברית ולזרעו והאמין בה'
ויחשבה לו צדקה . וכרת לו ברית בין עשר
אצבעות רגליו והיא ברית המילה, ועשר
אצבעות ידיו והוא הלשון . וקשר לו עשרים
ושתים אותיות בלשונו וגלה לו את יסודן .
משכן במים דלקם באש רעשן ברוח בערן
בשבעה נהגם בשנים עשר מזלות :

tenth is the furthest from the source and is thus the least spiritual.

2. *They are like the skin of onions.* The outer sphere encloses the inner. The outer is like a peel (*klipah*) to the inner. The inner is like the marrow (*mo'ach*) to the outer. In this metaphor, the inner is the greater (more spiritual).

3. *They form the shape of a man.* They stand in three columns—three *Sefirot* represent the right side of the body, three the left, and four the middle. The different kabbalistic schools deal differently with the reconciliation of these differing structures.

The concepts of Kabbalah are couched in everyday physical terms like light and flows, but they refer to spiritual ideas of a completely different nature.

Moses Cordovero says that all three are valid ways of describing different aspects of the *Sefirot*. Thus, one above the other stresses the superiority of the emanator over the emanated. The prior *Sefirah* is the cause of the others and is thus represented as higher. The second is emanated from the first and is thus lower. At the same time it is the cause of the third and is consequently higher.

The second structure (the Onion Model) is meant to show that the same *Sefirah* can be described as important (marrow) or less important (peel), depending on the relationship. Each is marrow to the other skins at the same time as they are peel to the inner layers. Finally, the third structure (three-column man-shaped model) stresses the individual aspects of each *Sefirah* in relationship to the others.

Thus, to Moses Cordovero, there is no contradiction among these three models. The *Sefirot* are not physical, and the different models are just a way to convey spiritual relationships. Sometimes one model is more appropriate for explaining a specific relationship

---

The Sefirot *are not physical, and the different models are just a way to convey spiritual relationships.*

---

than another. Lurian Kabbalah adopts a different approach. Chaim Vital, the main expounder of Lurian Kabbalah, says in his main work, *Etz Chaim*, that in different worlds different structures apply. Thus, in the world known as the World of Dots, the *Sefirot* are one above the other; in other worlds they are in circles and in columns.

The model that has been used most frequently is the three-column man-shaped one. The *Sefirot* on the right represent attributes of kindness (*chesed*), those on the left represent strictness (*din*), and the middle ones mediate between the left and right. The ten *Sefirot* have flows of spiritual matter between them, flowing through what are known in the kabbalistic physical metaphor as "pipes" (*tzinorot*). There are twenty-two of these "pipes," from which are derived the twenty-two letters of the Hebrew alphabet.

The first *Mishnah* in *Sefer Yetzirah* states, "He created his world with book, number, and story." By this is meant that the elements of language and math were combined in such a way as to create a story — not any story, but the story of creation.

It must be pointed out that what is meant by letters is clearly more than mere elements of language. The Raivad says in his glosses to *Mishneh Torah* that all languages are translations of reality, except for the Holy Tongue, which is the language of reality itself, that is, the Hebrew letters of "chair" represent the powers that give chairs their real world existence. The English word "chair," on the other hand, is merely a convenient way to refer to a chair. So it is these powers, represented by the Hebrew alphabet, that are referred to by *Sefer Yetzirah* as the basic building blocks with which the world was created.

Perhaps even more esoteric is the other main group of elements in *Sefer Yetzirah*, the numbers. The source for the numbers are the *Sefirot*. The word "*Sefirah*" in Hebrew comes from the same root as number, "*sefor*." It refers to the ten emanations of God's light. It is these emanations that are responsible for the diversity in the world.

From *The Fundamentals of Jewish Mysticism: The Book of Creation and Its Commentaries*.

Leonard R. Glotzer received a Bachelor of Arts degree in psychology from Brooklyn College and rabbinic ordination from Yeshivat Eretz Yisroel in New York. He served as rabbi of the New Springville Synagogue in Staten Island from 1976 to 1982.

VI
The Ten Sefirot

12

The Ten Sefirot

Y. David Shulman

The first *sefirah* is called *Keter*: "crown." It is the most transcendent of *sefirot*, closest to the blazing, inconceivable light of the Infinite One.

Then the light of *Keter* is filtered down to the second *sefirah, Chochmah*: "wisdom." *Chochmah* is the incipient flash of what the structure of this world will be.

From *Chochmah* comes *Binah*: "understanding." *Binah* is the broadening and development of that primal flash of insight.

The culmination of *Chochmah* and *Binah* is *Da'at*: "knowledge." Because *Keter* is so exalted and hidden, it is sometimes not counted as a *sefirah*. In that case, *Da'at* is counted. *Da'at* represents the union and integration of *Chochmah* and *Binah*. Now the balanced flow of Divine energy can proceed.

The next *sefirah* is *Chesed*: "lovingkindness." A much more tangible form of creation is taking place. This first step is an untrammeled outpouring of limitless love.

This is balanced by *Gevurah*: "might." This is the *sefirah* of holding back and constriction. It is a necessary placing of boundaries on the exuberant force of a loving creation.

These two forces are integrated and balanced in the following *sefirah* of *Tiferet*: "beauty." Now love and withholding are in balance, with a slight tilt toward love.

After this comes *Netzach*: "victory." This is again, on a more tangible plane, a *sefirah* of giving. This time, the giving is one of overpowering and overcoming.

Netzach must be balanced by *Hod*: "glory." *Hod* is related to *Gevurah*. It is more gentle, a receiving openness to Divine energy.

These two *sefirot*, of *Netzach* and *Hod*, combine in *Yesod*: "foundation." Foundation is the conduit for all the *sefirot* above it. Through it, like water through a

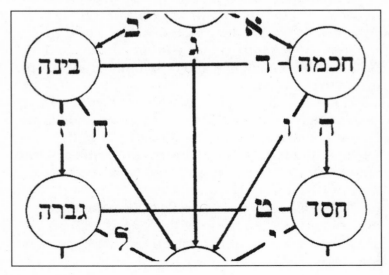

sluice, energy flows down in a directed stream. It is a holy energy that must be directed and controlled wisely. Therefore, it is analogous to human sexuality.

The final *sefirah* is *Malchut*: "kingdom." This *sefirah*, which has received the energy of all those above it, rules the world over which it hangs and which it permeates.

Each one of these *sefirot* has a wealth of characteristics, and can be known by many names.

Besides this, the *sefirot* interact in a complex set of relationships.

A primal dynamic is the balance between male and female energies. The *sefirot* can be arranged in three

---

A primal dynamic is the balance between male and female energies.

---

columns. The right-hand column is male, the left-hand female, and the middle column blends the two.

The paradigm of the *sefirot* is repeated infinitely, one set within another.

Imagine a series of infinite universes. At the very bottom is our own world, with its billions of galaxies, each containing billions of stars, spanning distances of billions of light years.

This universe is merely a small part of the more spiritual universe directly above it. Creation rises, level after level, in a scope of unfathomable greatness. The higher universes contain a profusion of spiritual energies that we can barely imagine, filled with spiritual beings and processes. Higher and higher do the universes ascend. And in each one, we are aware of the progressively more powerful flow of divine energy coursing down.

We rise from level to level, like explorers tracing the source of a mighty river. Finally, we come to a level that totally baffles us, that overwhelms our most evolved and purified spiritual being. It is as though we stand beneath a roaring, battering, brilliant Niagara Falls of overpowering spiritual energy. All our thoughts and conceptions, our consciousness and awareness, are shattered. We have come to the limit of any created being to understand Godliness. Beyond this is the great source of Being that created beings can experience only as an exalted Nothingness.

And the energy that flows through all these universes is the dynamic flow of processes running in a complex and never-ending interplay of balanced, interacting energies and vessels. These are the *sefirot*.

The Jewish mystical tradition teaches that even this conception is a corporealization of processes that transcend human intellect. In the upper worlds, there is neither space nor time. Therefore, all the words and concepts used to describe the *sefirot* are hopelessly impoverished.

Just as a poem can recreate the mood of a magnificent vision, so can the descriptions of *sefirot* provide a taste of the spiritual world that flows above and about us.

From *The Sefirot: Ten Emanations of Divine Power*.

Y. David Shulman is the author of *Chambers of the Palace: Teachings of Rabbi Nachman of Bratslav*. He has written historical biographies of figures such as Rashi, Maimonides, the Maharal of Prague, and the Vilna Gaon. He has also translated the travel letters of Rabbi Ovadiah of Bartenura (*Pathway to Jerusalem*).

13

The Sefirot and the Days of Creation

Adin Steinsaltz

The Torah speaks "the language of man" in order for man to understand it in such a way that is at least able to relate to it with the ordering of his life (if not with his mind). It is also the primordial design, the archetypal metaphor whose origin is God Himself. From this point, the giving of the Torah is like God's gift of Himself to man. It may be regarded as the permeation of the inconceivably great into the circumscribed

---

The giving of the Torah is like God's gift of Himself to man.

---

domain of the human. But the only way for men to comprehend it is through allegory and metaphor. By such means, the human mind can make leaps and build bridges to overcome the abyss in some pragmatic way. This has been done by the "scholars of Truth," the sages of the Kabbalah.

For example: These scholars of Truth have called the Sefirot "lights" to help us understand the nature of the unity of God and His attributes. For actually, the distance between God and the Divine attributes is too great for us to cross; all our ordinary comparisons and standards are woefully inadequate. Moreover, in the higher worlds, the essence of all things is so much greater and more varied than anything we can conceive, and the difference between levels of existence so much more pronounced that we cannot consider even the possibility of a relationship that can overcome the vastness of the gap. All that we can have any idea about, as said, is based on the Secret of Faith, on the

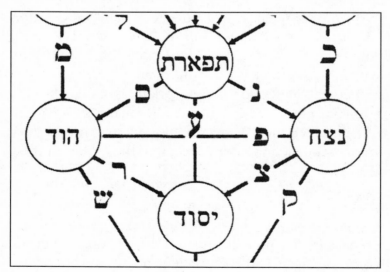

premise that, in a manner we cannot fathom, God does unite with the Sefirot and acts through them. And since permission has been granted to speak of the Sefirot by the use of allegory and metaphor, we are able to obtain a certain insight into the relations between the human and the Divine in the world.

To return to our kabbalistic example of calling the Sefirot "lights," the metaphorical image is that of the light of the sun and sun itself. Before it goes forth from the globe of the sun, the light is an inextinguishable part of the sun and has neither name nor existence. Only when it is separated from its source does this radiation become something in itself, identifiable as sunlight. As it is written, "And God called the light — day" (Genesis 1:5). This metaphor (of sun and sunlight) has already appeared in our dissertation, but whereas previously it was intended to portray the nullification of creaturely existence in the Creator, here the intention is to show the unity of the Sefirot with God. It is appropriate only in that it helps to see the relation between the Sefirot and their Divine source and to illustrate how the "Secret of Faith," although it transcends reason, can be grasped by the mind.

To pursue the image further, just as the light of the sun becomes visible to us only upon separating from the sun, so too do the Sefirot exist for us only when they issue from the World of Emanation. Before that, they are still united in the one Divine reality. (But, it must be repeated, the image is inadequate; no words or metaphors can do more than express our limitedness, to "enable the ear to hear what it can understand.") The Sefirot are emanated and assume their separate identities to our consciousness; at the same time we are contained in them and guided by them.

Just as Genesis is a creation of a world out of nothing, so too are the Ten Sefirot called forth out of God to direct hidden worlds and revealed worlds, for as it is said in the Introduction to *Tikunei Zohar*: "You conceal yourself in them." God clothes Himself in the Sefirot in order to sustain the world He has created and to control its course. And since it is in the nature of a garment to both reveal and to hide, so too do the Sefirot reveal God's action and conceal it. Through our dim cognition of the Sefirot, we become aware of the way God directs us and our world.

Thus on the first day of Creation, the attribute of *Chesed* (Grace, Loving-kindness) was revealed. This is in accordance with the kabbalistic view that each of the seven days of Genesis marked the manifestation of another of the lower Sefirot, and on the first day it was Chesed. To be sure, all of the Sefirot are manifested in every process or phenomenon, and therefore they would all be present on the first day. This is what is known as "Partzuf" (Countenance), the whole experience in which each of the Sefirot contributes its feature to comprise a living face. Moreover, since each of the Sefirot includes all of the others, the attribute (Sefirah) of Chesed, which is the special revelation of the first day of Creation, is Chesed as a generality, including the other Sefirot in various combinations: *Keter* (Will), *Chochmah* (Wisdom), *Binah* (Understanding), *Daat* (Knowledge), and so on.

～

With Chesed He created the light through the utterance, "Let there be light" (Genesis 1:3). And the light was diffused from one end of the world to the other. Which spreading and diffusion and revealing of light streaming around and into all of reality is the attribute of Chesed. Because, as we may readily observe, the light of the first day is not the light of the sun (which was created only on the fourth day). Chesed, the "light of seven days," is another sort of light; it is a light that suffuses the whole of creation without limit, from one end of the world to the other.

However, as we have said, the attribute of Chesed does not manifest in its purity on the first day as that which is only Chesed; it comprises something of the other Sefirot as well, in particular the attribute of Gevurah. This attribute of contraction and the restriction of force and substance within limits is absolutely necessary for Chesed, which knows no such limits. If Chesed were to try to manifest pure and infinite in its power of giving, it would not be able to be "clothed in" (operating through) this world, which is finite and everywhere confined in its physicality. Therefore, too, the light of the first day is not spiritual in the absolute sense, like the supernal light; it has to be able to establish connections with this world. This is possible through the action of the second attribute of Gevurah within Chesed itself.

"In like manner, on the second day of Creation, the attribute of Gevurah was revealed." Here, too, since all of the Sefirot are included in each of the Sefirot, Strength too was not manifested in its purity, in its Almighty power; it necessarily had to include Chesed

(Loving-kindness) and various combinations of the other Sefirot. And with this was created the firmament with the Divine utterance, "Let there be a firmament in the midst of the waters and let it divide the waters from the waters" (Genesis 1:6). The action of Gevurah was to separate and divide and fix limits. And the creation

---

All of the Sefirot are included in each of the Sefirot.

---

of a firmament was not only a matter of fixing a radius for the sky, a parting of the waters above and below. It was the act of primordial division between the higher and the lower, with the firmament acting as a sort of fixed frontier in the created universe between the spiritual creatures of the heavens (upper waters) and the material creatures of the earth (lower waters). The "lower waters" are the primordial stuff out of which all the substantial things below are made, the earth and all that is on it, whereas the "upper waters" above the firmament are the essence and the source of all the spiritual things, at all their very many levels. The creation of the firmament is thus the establishment of the original barrier between the spiritual and the material, between "above" and "below."

This division is obviously not just a formal one of categories—it is a division that determines the very essence of all things—because in fixing the spiritual as a separate entity and the material as another entity, the effect is to sensitize the spiritual and to coarsen the material. Since all material substance is set into a world of its own, in an environment that is physical and

dense, it tends to become ever more inert and unre-
sponsive. The same is true of the spiritual in the opposite direction — it tends to become rarer and more
refined in its own higher realm.

However, as said, Gevurah does not manifest as a
single, pure attribute with sharp limitations; it has to
contain something of the attribute of Chesed at least,
for the world is build with Chesed (Psalm 89:3). The
resolute action of forming a barrier between the upper
and the lower worlds is actually a necessary step in the
process of creating the earth, it physicality and fertility,
its ability to give birth to new forms, new life. It is from
the earth that man was created and it is from the earth
that man draws sustenance to exist and to fulfil the
purpose for which he was formed. The Gevurah that is
the chief manifestation of the second day thus has

---

*It is from the earth that man was created and it is
from the earth that man draws sustenance to exist
and to fulfil the purpose for which he was formed.*

---

within itself also Chesed and the other Sefirot needed
to break out of changelessness and rigidity and to
establish the groundwork for "Chesed to build the
world." At the same time, of course, there is a clear
distinction between the first day and the second day,
between the gracious giving without stint and the
defining of boundaries to this benevolence; the second
is needed in order for everything to find its place, the
material to the material, the spiritual to the spiritual.
The formation of the elemental barrier between upper
and lower worlds is indeed primary; from this moment

it becomes virtually impossible to cross over from one to the other.

Similarly for all the other seven days of Creation and the Sefirah characteristic of each, what happens is a combination of forces that makes for a living and creatively dynamic reality. Thus the third day is in the sign of Tiferet (Splendor, Harmony, Mercy), which is the attribute blending its two predecessors, Chesed and Gevurah. It has the advantage of both of these, the wideness of the sea and the charm of place on the land; it expresses both the harmony of their multiplicity in Creation and the vigorousness that is necessary for individual growth. As it is said in *Tikunei Zohar*: "Tiferet shows how the world is conducted with righteousness and justice, (for) righteousness is law, justice is mercy." Both law and mercy are required for social justice and the ordering of human relations. Indeed, Chesed of itself, the act of love and of giving without limit, could prove disastrous if it is not controlled by duly considering the needs of the receiver. And this consideration is essentially compassion or mercy, the attribute of Tiferet. After all, justice is not merely the exacting of punishment or the passing of a verdict; it is also a matter of weighing all the factors involved, balancing the mitigating evidence, and so on. For the sin itself is beyond correction, at least as far as the act is concerned, and only the consequences can be related to. In such manner, true judgment comes to direct the course of the sentence. For law only distinguishes between good and evil, right and wrong; judgment is the proper use of mercy.

This substantiates the truth that the purpose of the

Sefirot is not only to conduct the affairs of the world but also to help the world. To be sure, the human values we somehow transfer to the Divine attributes are very different from their actual meaning, so that what we consider to be just from our point of view may not be the same as the Divine Tiferet and what we feel to be merciful may not be quite the same as what God intended. Nevertheless, we are convinced that God acts with justice and mercy in everything, even when we cannot understand it on any level. The point is that we cannot grasp the attributes on any other level but our own; the explanations we give are not able to define God's real Essence and Being. It is simply that through them He measures us; they are the mode by which God makes all things happen in the limited reality within which we exist and to which we respond.

From *The Sustaining Utterance: Discourses on Chasidic Thought.*

Rabbi Adin Steinsaltz, scholar, teacher, mystic, scientist, and social critic, is internationally regarded as one of the leading rabbis of this century. The author of many books, he is best known for his monumental translation of and commentary on the Talmud. In 1988, Rabbi Steinsaltz was awarded the Israel Prize, his country's highest honor. He and his family live in Jerusalem.

VII
Meditation and Kabbalah

14

Meditation and Kabbalah

Aryeh Kaplan

Meditation is primarily a means of attaining liberation. Its various methods are designated to loosen the bond of the physical, allowing the individual to ascend to the transcendental, spiritual realm. One who accomplishes this successfully is said to have attained *Ruach HaKodesh*, The "Holy Spirit," which is the general Hebraic term for enlightenment.

The best-known contemporary method of meditation is that which involves a mantra, a word or phrase that is repeated over and over for a designated period of time. One concentrates on the mantra to the exclusion of all else, thus clearing the mind of all extraneous thoughts and divorcing it from the normal stream of consciousness. In this method, the mantra may be repeated verbally, or the repetition may be completely mental. This type of meditation is found in the Kabbalah, especially among the earlier schools. In the *Hekhalot*, for example, one begins his spiritual ascent by repeating a number of Divine Names 112 times.

Mantra meditation is an example of structured, externally directed meditation. It is externally directed, insofar as one concentrates on a word or phrase, rather than on the spontaneous thoughts to the mind. Since it involves a specific practice, repeated for a fixed length of time, it is considered a structured meditation.

Another example of structured externally-directed meditation is contemplation, where one gazes at an object, placing all of one's concentration on it. In occult practices, the best-known type of contemplation involves gazing into a crystal ball. Other types of contemplation involve mandalas, pictures or letter designs, where one gazes upon them, emptying the mind of all other thoughts. In Kabbalah meditation, the simplest contemplative device is the Tetragrammaton itself, and this is discussed even in non-kabbalistic works. More complex forms are also used, and this

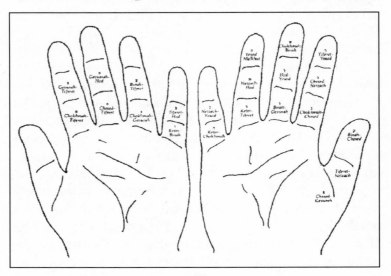

method seems to have reached its zenith under the influence of Rabbi Shalom Sharabi (1702–1777).

In Kabbalah meditation, the simplest contemplative device is the Tetragrammaton itself, and this is discussed even in non-kabbalistic works.

Very closely related to this is the method of *Yechu-dim* (Unifications), which plays an important role in the system of the Ari. Here one does not contemplate a physical picture, but rather a mental image, usually consisting of various combinations of divine names. Since the structures and combinations of these names are predetermined, and do not arise spontaneously in the mind, this is also considered to be an externally-directed meditation.

The second basic method of meditation is that which is internally-directed. This consists of meditating on thoughts, feelings or mental images that arise spontaneously in the mind. Usually, this is best accomplished by focusing on a general area, around which these thoughts will be evoked. Since there is no formal or predetermined method of evoking such thoughts, this is most commonly an unstructured meditation.

Internally-directed meditation can be practiced purely in thought, or, as in some systems, one's thoughts can also be verbalized. One of the best methods of verbalizing such thoughts while keeping them concentrated on a single focus is to express them as spontaneous prayer. It is this method that forms the basis for the meditative system of Rabbi Nachman of Breslov.

The third basic type of meditation is that which is non-directed. Such meditation strives for a stillness of the mind and a withdrawal from all perception, both internal and external. It plays an important role in the advanced states of many other methods, but at the same time, it can also be used as a method in its own right. Very little is expressly written about this method, but it appears to play a role in the teachings of such Hasidic masters as Rabbi Dov Baer, the Maggid of Mezrich (1704–1772) and Rabbi Levi Yitzchak of Berdichov (1740–1809).

There is evidence that this method was used, at least for the most advanced, in the very terminology of

---

The Kabbalists call the highest level of transcendence Ayin, *literally "Nothingness."*

---

the Kabbalah. Indeed, in a number of cases, it is only when looked upon in this sense that some terminology is comprehensible. Thus, for example, the Kabbalists call the highest level of transcendence *Ayin*, literally "Nothingness." Actually, this alludes to the ultimate level reached by non-directed meditation, where all perception and imagery cease to exist.

~

Besides being divided into these three basic methods, meditation can be classified according to the means used. The three basic means are the intellect, the emotions, and the body.

The path of the intellect is very prevalent among the theoretical Kabbalists, and was also used outside of the kabbalistic schools. The most common method was simply to contemplate on various aspects of the Torah, probing the inner meaning of its commandments. It also included delving deeply with the intellect into the structure of the supernal universes, and, as it were, becoming a denizen of these worlds. For many, this method leads to a very high state of ecstasy, and this method forms the basis of the Habad system of Hasidism.

Another form of intellectual meditation involves the study of devotional works, carefully contemplating each concept in an effort to attain self-improvement. It was primarily this method that formed the basis of the Mussar Movement, which arose in the Nineteenth Century as a response to Hasidism. Such contemplation, or *Hitbonenut*, plays an especially important role in the devotional work *Mesilat Yesharim* (Path of the Just), by the great Kabbalist Rabbi Moshe Chaim Luzzatto (1707–1747). In this remarkable book, the author outlines all the steps leading up to, but not including, *Ruach HaKodesh* the ultimate enlightenment. The method of attaining these desired traits is that of *Hitbonenut*—contemplation on the teachings germain to that step and rectifying one's life in the light of these teachings. Incidentally, although it is not widely known, the ten levels discussed in this text clearly parallel the ten mystical *Sefirot* of the Kabbalists.

The path of the emotions also plays an important role in the systems of the Kabbalists. One place where it is particularly important is in *Kavanah*-meditation, the system that makes use of the formal daily prayers as a sort of mantra, especially in the Hasidic schools. Here one is taught to place all of his feelings and emotions into the words of his worship, thus attaining a divestment of the physical (*hitpashtut hagashmiut*). This path is also found in meditations involving music, which played an important role in the meditations of the ancient prophets of the Bible.

A path combining the intellect and emotions is the path of love, described in detail by the leading philosopher, Rabbi Moses Maimonides (1135–1204). He writes that when a person deeply contemplates on God, thinking of His mighty deeds and wondrous creations, he becomes profoundly aware of His wisdom, and is brought to a passionate love for God. He speaks of a level of love called *Cheshek* (passion), where the emotion is so intense that every thought is exclusively engaged with its object. This love for God can be so intense that the soul can literally be drawn out of the body by it, and this is what occurs when a saint dies by the "Kiss of God." This is considered to be one of the highest possible levels of enlightenment, usually attained only at very advanced age.

The third path is that of the body. It includes both the body motions and breathing exercizes that play a key role in the system of Rabbi Abraham Abulafia. The swaying and bowing that accompanies formal prayer also involves the path of the body, enhancing the meditative quality of the worship.

One of the most important techniques of body meditation involves dancing. This is especially true among the Hasidic schools, where even after other meditative methods were abandoned, dance was still used as a means of attaining ecstasy and enlightenment. This, however, was not a Hasidic innovation, since

Even in most ancient times dance was an important method for attaining enlightenment.

even in most ancient times dance was an important method for attaining enlightenment.

The Talmud teaches that on the festival of Succot (Tabernacles), during the "Festival of Drawing," in Jerusalem, "saints and men of deed would dance before the assemblage, holding torches and singing hymns of praise." This festival was a particularly propitious time for attaining enlightenment, as the Jerusalem Talmud states, "Why was it called a 'Festival of Drawing'? Because it was a time when people drew in *Ruach HaKodesh*." So closely was dance associated with enlightenment, that the Future World, which is viewed as the ultimate place of enlightenment, is described as "A dance conducted by the Blessed Holy One, where each individual points a finger at Him."

One reason why so little is known about the various systems of Kabbalah meditation is that all of this literature is in Hebrew, and it has never been accurately translated. Since most of these methods are no longer practiced, the vocabulary associated with them has also been forgotten. So great is this confusion that even the very Hebrew word for meditation is not generally known. This has even led to the use of the wrong term in an article on the subject in a major Judaic encyclopedia. Once a basic vocabulary is established, however, one can gain an appreciation of how often meditation is discussed in classical texts, particularly in the kabbalistic classics.

There is one word that is consistently used as a term for meditation by the commentators, philosophers and Kabbalists. The word which most often denotes meditation is *Hitbodedut*. The verb, "to meditate," is represented by the word *Hitboded*.

The word *Hitboded* is derived from the root *Badad* (???), meaning "to be secluded." Literally, then, *Hitbodedut* actually means self-isolation, and in some cases, actually refers to nothing more than physical seclusion and isolation. In many other places, however, it is used to denote a state of consciousness involving the isolation of the self, that is, the isolation of the individual's most basic essence.

Thus, when discussed in a kabbalistic context, the word *Hitbodedut* means much more than mere physical isolation. It refers to a state of internal isolation, where the individual mentally secludes his essence from his thoughts. One of the greatest Kabbalists,

---

When discussed in a kabbalistic context, the word Hitbodedut *means much more than mere physical isolation. It refers to a state of internal isolation, where the individual mentally secludes his essence from his thoughts.*

Rabbi Chaim Vital (1543–1620), often spoke of such mental seclusion, saying that "one must seclude himself (*hitboded*) in his thoughts to the ultimate degree." In doing this, one separates his soul from his body to such a degree that he no longer feels any relationship to his physical self. The soul is thus isolated, and as Rabbi Chaim Vital concludes, "the more one separates himself from the physical, the greater will be his enlightenment."

This state of mental seclusion is very important to the prophetic experience. The clearest description of this state is presented by Rabbi Levi ben Gershon (1288–1344), a major Jewish philosopher, often known as Gersonides, or simply by the acrostic, "the Ralbag." He writes that the attainment of prophetic revelation "requires the isolation (*hitbodedut*) of the consciousness from the imagination, or both of these from the other perceptive mental faculties."

Rabbi Isaac of Acco also uses the same definition. Speaking of individuals seeking prophecy, he writes, "They fulfil the conditions of meditation (*Hitbodedut*) which has the effect of nullifying the senses and divorcing the thought processes of the soul from all perception, clothing it in the spiritual essence of the transcendental."

One of the clearest expressions of this has been developed by Rabbi Abraham Maimonides (1186–1237), son of the famed Moses Maimonides. He writes that there are two different types of self-isolation (*hitbodedut*), external and internal. External *hitbodedut* is nothing more than physical isolation, and this is usually desirable when one wishes to meditate. Internal *hitbodedut*, on the other hand, consists of isolating the soul from the perceptive faculty. When the mind is completely hushed in this manner, one becomes able to perceive the spiritual realm.

The word *Hitbodedut* therefore primarily is used to

denote the isolation of the soul or ego from all external and internal stimuli. Any method of practice that is used to accomplish this is also called *Hitbodedut*. Since these are the practices that are usually referred to as "meditation," this is how the word *Hitbodedut* should be translated.

Another closely related term, *Hitbonenut*, is also often translated as "meditation." (Indeed, this is the term used in the above-mentioned encyclopedia article.) From context, however, we see that a more precise definition of *Hitbodedut* is "contemplation," that is, intense concentration on an object or image. Of course, contemplation is a meditative technique, but it is significant to note that the term is hardly ever used in the classical Kabbalah texts in describing the attainment of the higher states of consciousness.

From *Meditation and Kabbalah*.

Rabbi Aryeh Kaplan was born in New York City and was educated in the Torah Voda'as and Mir Yeshivot in Brooklyn. After years of study at Jerusalem's Mir Yeshiva, he was ordained by some of Israel's foremost rabbinic authorities. He also earned a master's degree in physics and was listed in *Who's Who in Physics in the United States*. In the course of a writing career spanning only twelve years, Rabbi Kaplan earned a reputation as one of the most effective, persuasive, scholarly, and prolific exponents of Judaism in the English language. He died on January 28, 1983, at the age of 48.

15

The Vocabulary of Kabbalistic Meditation

Aryeh Kaplan

In all kabbalistic literature, it is taken for granted that Divine Names play an important role in attaining the mystical state. In the Bible itself, however, there is no explicit mention of the use of such Names, except for some enticing hints. Thus, in a number of places, we find that an individual prophesies "in the name *(Ba-Shem)* of God." As anyone familiar with Hebrew will readily see, this can just as easily be translated as prophesying "*with* the name of God." These phrases would then speak of using God's name as a means of attaining the prophetic state.

Some Kabbalists also see the use of God's name as a method of attaining enlightenment in the case of Abraham. The Bible says that "he called in the name of God"

(Genesis 12:8). This is usually interpreted to mean that he prayed in God's name, or announced God's existence to the world, but the kabbalistic interpretation fits the words more literally.

A very similar interpretation is given to the verse, "He was enraptured in Me, and I will bring him forth. I will raise him up because he knew My name" *(Psalms 91:14)*. Here, a major commentator, Rabbi Abraham Ibn Ezra (1089–1164), states explicitly that this means that "he knew the mystery of My name." An ancient Midrash likewise states in the name of the great sage of the second century, Rabbi Pinchas ben Yair, "Why do people pray without being answered? Because they do not know how to use the Explicit Name *(Shem HaMeforesh)*." Since this Midrash is expounding the above verse, it is a clear indication that "knowing God's name" implies knowing how to actually make use of it.

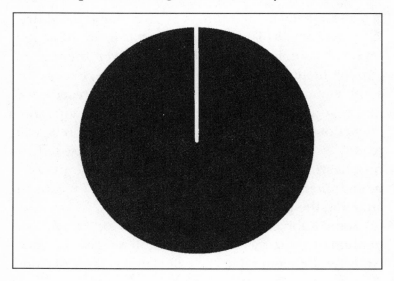

There are other hints of the power of God's Name. The Psalmist thus says, "Some come with chariots, some with horses, but we utter the name of God" *(Psalms 20:8)*. The usual interpretation is that this is speaking of prayer, but here too, the verse can be taken literally. This is particularly suggested by a verse that introduces this concept: "We will ecstasize *(Ranen)* in Your salvation, and in (with) the Name of God, we will ascend, God will fill all your requests" *(Psalms 20:6)*. As we shall see, the Hebrew word *Ranen* refers to a method of meditation, and here we see that it also involves God's Name. A very similar concept is found in the verse, "All nations surround me, but with the name of God I will destroy them with a word" *(Psalms 118:10)*.

The tradition regarding these Names of God is well established in the Talmud, and is discussed in many places. Most prominent are the various names that the Bible uses for God, and these are found to be ten in number, paralleling the Ten Sefirot. Besides this, the Talmud also speaks of a Name containing twelve letters, as well as one containing forty-two, both of which are described in kabbalistic literature. There is also considerable discussion of a Name containing seventy-two letters or triads, and this plays an important role, especially in Abulafia's system. The Talmud is filled with traditions regarding the power of these names when they are properly used.

The most important and potent of God's names is the Tetragrammaton, YHVH. This name is never pronounced out loud, even in prayer. It is taught that one who pronounces the Tetragrammaton disrespectfully is guilty of a most serious offense, and is worthy of death.

Although the Tetragrammaton is often discussed with respect to kabbalistic meditation, the Kabbalists likewise warn against pronouncing it out loud. The eminent Kabbalist, Rabbi Moshe Cordevero, writes, "If one wishes to utter the Tetragrammaton, he should do so with his mouth closed, so that no air should leave his mouth. It should not be voiced at all, but only mouthed with the larynx and tongue. Among initiates, this method is known as 'swallowing' the Divine Name." Even this, however, should not be done except when one reaches the highest disciplines of meditation.

Although the Tetragrammaton is often discussed with respect to kabbalistic meditation, the Kabbalists likewise warn against pronouncing it out loud.

The Talmud teaches that the only place where it was ever permitted to actually pronounce the Tetragrammaton was in the Holy Temple *(Bet HaMikdash)* in Jerusalem. This is based on the verse which calls the Temple "The place that God will choose . . . to place His Name there" *(Deuteronomy 12:5)*. Since the prophets apparently made use of the Tetragrammaton in attaining the mystical state, they would most often meditate in one of the chambers of the Holy Temple.

The main place where the Tetragrammaton was publicly used was in the Temple, for the Priestly Blessing, as well as ten times during the public confessions of the Yom Kippur service. Whenever this Name was pronounced during a Temple service, all present would respond, "Blessed be the name of His glorious Kingdom forever and ever."

On Yom Kippur, those standing near the front would also prostrate themselves to the ground, in awe and reverence of God's most holy Name. There is a Talmudic tradition that one of the miracles of the Holy Temple was that they had room to prostrate themselves, even though they stood tightly packed together during the service.

Originally, the Tetragrammaton was used by all the priests in the Priestly Blessing in the Temple. The Talmud teaches, however, that after the death of Simon the Just (around 291 B.C.E.), its use was discontinued, since the Divine presence was no longer manifest in the Temple, and the other priests felt themselves unworthy. As long as the Temple stood, however, it was used by the High Priest in the Yom Kippur service, but it was repeated so low that it was drowned out by the singing of the other priests. All this was so that those who were unworthy should not learn precisely how it is to be pronounced.

There is some discussion in the literature as to why all these Names have such a profound effect. Rabbi Abraham Abulafia states that the Names themselves do not have any intrinsic powers, but rather, when properly used, can induce states of consciousness where the person himself has such powers. The Name is therefore used primarily as a meditative device to bring the individual into certain states of consciousness, transporting him to the proper spiritual framework, whether for prophecy or to direct spiritual energy in other ways.

Most Kabbalists, however, maintain that besides this, the Names also have important intrinsic power. They are intimately attached to various spiritual Forces, and when one makes proper use of these Names, these Forces are brought into play and one can bind himself to them. Since all the Divine Names are extremely potent in this respect, one must be extremely careful not to use them except in the proper context and in the most serious manner.

One of the greatest sources of confusion is the fact that many people think that these Names need only to be recited to be effective. According to all the kabbalistic texts that speak of this, use of the Divine Names involves much more than this. First, there is considerable preparation that the individual requires before he can make use of these Names. The Names themselves, in most cases, were used very much like a mantra. In the *Hekhalot,* a mystical text dating from the first century, we find certain Names and letter combinations which must be repeated over and over, bringing the user into the mystical state. In other cases, they were repeated in combination with other letters, with an entire series of different vowel points. Abulafia's system calls for this, and also includes various body motions and breathing techniques. When used as *Yechudim* (Unifications), letters of various Names had to be contemplated with deep concentration and brought together in various ways.

While the Divine Names could help a person reach a meditative state when used correctly, their use had to be preceded by considerable spiritual preparation. Most important were the Ten Steps leading to *Ruach HaKodesh* discussed earlier. It is only after one has attained these Ten Steps through intense self discipline that these meditative methods can be truly effective. If one is not sufficiently prepared, he may indeed attain "enlightenment," but it will be from a source far removed from the holy.

In general, then, the proper use of the various Divine Names was seen as the key to prophecy and

---

This was also one of the most closely guarded secrets of the Kabbalah.

---

enlightenment. At the same time, this was also one of the most closely guarded secrets of the Kabbalah.

From *Meditation and the Bible*.

Rabbi Aryeh Kaplan was born in New York City and was educated in the Torah Voda'as and Mir Yeshivot in Brooklyn. After years of study at Jerusalem's Mir Yeshiva, he was ordained by some of Israel's foremost rabbinic authorities. He also earned a master's degree in physics and was listed in *Who's Who in Physics in the United States*. In the course of a writing career spanning only twelve years, Rabbi Kaplan earned a reputation as one of the most effective, persuasive, scholarly, and prolific exponents of Judaism in the English language. He died on January 28, 1983, at the age of 48.

16

The Purpose and Practice of Meditation

Steven A. Fisdel

"The beginning of Wisdom is Awe of the Lord. All who practice them (the Ways of Wisdom) have great understanding. Praise of Him stands for eternity" (Psalm 111:20).

What the Psalmist is saying so eloquently summarizes the core purpose of Jewish meditation practice. True wisdom is not knowledge. Nor is it comprehension or understanding per se. Wisdom is Knowingness. It is being so closely connected with something at its core level that you are experiencing its light firsthand. There is nothing to know in the cognitive sense. There are no questions and there are no answers. You truly know, because you experience connection and unification. Such direct experience is beyond the level of mind. Rather, it is a direct melding of light with light.

The ultimate objective of meditation in Jewish tradition is to achieve and maintain this direct connection with God and to reach unification with the Light of His Presence in the universe. This is referred to by the Hebrew term *devekut*. This is adhesion to God through direct experience. It is achieved by focus. It is maintained by devotion. The experience is Knowingness.

To achieve Wisdom, one has to practice the Ways of Wisdom. Practicing the Ways of Wisdom involves study, discipline, consistent moral behavior, prayer, devotion, and meditation. The two general terms for meditation in Hebrew point directly to the purpose of meditation and its extreme importance. The terms are *Hitbodedut* and *Hitbonenut*.

Hitbodedut literally means "to be by oneself," "to be completely alone." This describes the reality of meditative practice and experience. When journeying

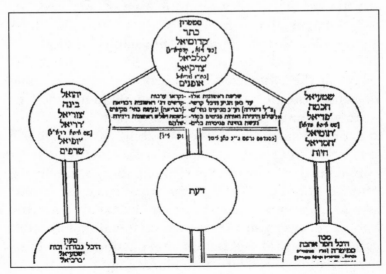

toward God, one may pass through multiple realms of reality and many levels of experience. However, one is making the journey alone. Meditation is an intimately personal, inward process. It is a sacred journey of the Self back toward God, the Source. It is the individual soul moving toward the Core of Being. It is the ultimate inner dialogue. It is a road of experience one travels alone.

The ultimate objective of meditation in Jewish tradition is to achieve and maintain this direct connection with God and to reach unification with the Light of His Presence in the universe.

The effect of pursuing this journey is a constant recurring one. It is reflected in the term, *Hitbonenut*, meaning "self-understanding," "knowing oneself." The continuing effect, the benefit and purpose of meditation, is the evolution of the Self, the growth and development of the Soul. One evolves by experiencing more and more, on higher and higher levels of existence.

Knowingness of oneself and Knowingness of God are interlocked. They are interactive and mutually supporting of each other. They are the source of the evolution of the soul and the expansion of consciousness. The path to Knowingness is conscious connection to God. The path to connection is meditation. The result of the process is the growth of soul and of consciousness. All who practice the Ways of Wisdom have true understanding. All who have true understanding, Knowingness, remain eternally connected to

God. "All who practice it [wisdom] have true understanding. Praise of God stands [endures] for Eternity"
(Psalm 111:10).

Wisdom, upon which the Universe is created, origi-
nates with the quickening of the soul. When a person
is overwhelmed by the majesty of God's work and
senses the wonder of that which cannot be expressed,
he feels near to the Creator. When one is overpowered
by the pure joy of Creation, and praise and blessing
become spontaneous, one is indeed close to the very
source of life. At that moment, one is standing at the
threshold of Wisdom.

Wisdom once approached must be pursued. Sens-
ing God's nearness should lead the soul to the desire to
seek out His love. When one explores the universe
around him, experiencing wonder and awe at its gran-
deur, he is giving profound praise to its Creator by the
very act of experience. The soul is standing in an
eternal moment in close proximity to God's unconditional love. One is at the gates of wisdom and before
him lie all of its paths.

～

The Ways of Wisdom are many, and they are profoundly deep. The Ways of Wisdom are the mystic
paths that lead to humility, compassion, self-awareness,
and spiritual growth. They are the pathways that connect all levels of reality. They comprise the roads that
lead to God's Presence. They are meant to be traveled.
As the Psalmist states quite clearly, one who practices
them will attain higher consciousness.

Wisdom's beginning point and its end objective are the same: awe of God, the process of eternal praise of the Creator by the soul. Awe of God, connection to the Source, elevates the soul to higher levels of reality, beyond time and space. Following the Ways of Wisdom is the path of spiritual evolution. Pursuing the path is one of action, of doing, and of practice.

What are the Ways of Wisdom? They are study, the practice of justice, meditation, and devotion. Through this course of action comes true inner understanding and spiritual development.

It is the practice of Kabbalah, the practices of meditation drawn from millennia of Wisdom, which will be examined and detailed in this work, for the pursuit of Wisdom, in the fullest sense, requires a thorough knowledge of and deep commitment to meditation and meditative practice. Meditation is the genuine vehicle for attaining Knowingness and for drawing close to God. To experience God and to know self is to praise God within the eternal moment. That is the path of self-evolution. It is the highest obligation of the Soul.

Jewish meditation emerges from the Kabbalah, the Jewish mystic tradition. The term "Kabbalah" itself is very important to understand fully. A complete understanding sheds valuable light on the nature and relevance of the various meditation practices to be discussed, and on their application to one's inner life and personal experience.

First and foremost, the term *Kabbalah* means "reception, receptivity," from the Hebrew verb root signifying to receive or to accept. Receiving involves experiencing. If one receives a gift, for example, one accepts not only the gift, but also the gratitude, respect, or love that prompted it, the spirit in which it was given.

First and foremost, the term "Kabbalah" means "reception, receptivity," from the Hebrew verb root signifying to receive or to accept.

What is received may be solicited or come unsolicited. One may receive in the mail either an item that was ordered or a letter from an old friend. Either way, the act of receiving is an act of acceptance and it involves the recipient in a process, in which he is a participant.

On a spiritual level, receiving is the terminus point. It is the end result of a process. It is the fulfillment. It is the completion. Nothing given really fully exists unless it is received. God sends Life Force through all of Creation. It is simultaneously being received by all Creation and sustaining Creation's very existence. God sends down goodness and it is accepted by all worlds. Man does good and it flows back through all worlds and is received by God. Generating, sending, and receiving are the ebb and flow by which the universe operates.

The more one is willing to open up and receive from above, the more one comes to experience higher realities and intensify the content of life and foster soul development. That is the objective of meditation and practice.

Receiving in its primal form is the reception of Life Force. The great Hasidic master, Rabbi Levi Yitzhak of Berditchev, taught that from the highest level of the universe, the level of Unconditional Love, comes the spiritual influx that sustains all worlds. This influx can be sent down by God to this world or brought down to it by humanity.

The former, that is the Divine influx being sent down, is an act of pure Grace. It is an act of mercy initiated by God out of His love and concern for the whole of Creation. This flow can be received two ways. The first is passively. The influx of Life Force simultaneously streams down, invigorates, and sustains existence at all times. We need do nothing in this regard. This is a continual and primary reality that lies exclusively under God's direction.

There is also an active, participatory route. Through meditation, we can consciously attune our energy and our souls to the influx. To do so is to consciously seek to accept and experience God's unconditional love. This act of intent and focus transforms the reception of God's will from a passive one to an active one. This inner transformation produces revelation. Though the initiation of Grace emanates from God, focusing the heart and soul on it in deep meditation transforms the flow of Life Force, opening up the internal reality, the inner meaning of God's love, and making it manifest.

How is that accomplished? Let us harken back to the revelation at Mount Sinai. The immediacy of God's Presence caused the skies to thunder and the Earth to quake. The natural world reacted physically. It did not simply receive passively. By the same token, Moses and the Israelites reacted affirmatively, declaring, "We will do and we will understand." Confronted with the intensity of God's Presence manifesting, the Israelites responded actively. Confrontation with God requires a response. That response produces revelation in the form of inner understanding.

Revelation on any level, group or individual, is the process of reaching, experiencing, and coming to understand the inner essence of what one receives from

---

Kabbalist meditation is the receiving of God's abundant flow and the active penetration of the Divine influx, allowing the soul to absorb its inner meaning.

God on a continual basis. It is a process that requires effort, clear focus, and the will to search. This process of revelation is the primary focus of Jewish meditation, the practice of Kabbalah. Kabbalist meditation is the receiving of God's abundant flow and the active penetration of the Divine influx, allowing the soul to absorb its inner meaning.

∼

In Kabbalah, the flow of energy that sustains the universe is dual in its direction. It flows both from the Source, God's Will, to the whole of Creation, and upon being received, Creation responds by sending energy back to God. This double flow is intrinsic, as the Kabbalah sees it. God's Grace and mankind's actions form a flow of energy, uniform in both directions.

This dual movement has particularly important implications in relation to humanity. Every time one receives, acts, and comes to understand what has been received, his energy can be channeled constructively. Energy and will can be directed outward toward creation as creativity or upward toward God, manifesting as devotion and resonance with His Will.

According to Levi Yitzhak, the ideal would be to focus one's intentions, actions, and consciousness on the pure joy that God has, when one seeks Him in love and clings to Him with devotion. This intensity opens the gates of Heaven and floods the soul, and indeed all worlds, with light, blessing, and inner peace, meditation being the key to such focus.

As one actively moves toward God, more and more light is received, more love is experienced, and more understanding is gained. Here, the soul is reintegrating with itself. It is healing itself and finding God in the process.

The process itself fosters an increasingly deep relationship. The process of seeking God, climbing the Tree of Life, is that of the evolving relationship between the soul and its source. As the relationship deepens, so does the joy. God rejoices at the effort. The soul is ecstatic about its increasing sense of Self and its growing closeness to the Creator. In summary, the basis of Kabbalah is receiving. However, receiving is not merely reception alone. It is equally receptivity.

Kabbalah is a three-part process. One which is both active and passive. First, one passively receives. Then, one acts on what has been received through doing, through meditation, through learning and teaching. Finally, by so asserting oneself actively, one becomes receptive to experiencing higher levels of reality, to reintegrating and healing the soul, and to returning to God.

From *The Practice of Kabbalah: Meditation in Judaism.*

Rabbi Steven Fisdel is the spiritual leader of Congregation Beth Israel in Chico, California. Based in the San Franciso Bay Area, Rabbi Fisdel maintains a private practice, counseling, lecturing, and teaching extensively in the areas of Kabbalah, spirituality, history, and mysticism. He is affiliated with Chochmat HaLev, an institute for Jewish learning in Berkeley, the Foundation for Mind Being Research in Los Altos, and several Bay Area colleges. Rabbi Fisdel was ordained by Zalman Schachter-Shalomi through the Pnai Or Foundation in Philadelphia and is a graduate of the Hebrew University in Jerusalem and of Spertus College of Judaica in Chicago. Rabbi Fisdel has spent more than twenty-five years in Jewish education as a teacher, educational administrator, congregational rabbi, and public speaker.

VIII
Selected Topics

17

Reincarnation

DovBer Pinson

Rabbi Hayim Vital illustrates in his book that the concept of reincarnation is not only an esoteric teaching whose prime source is the Kabbalah, in the revealed parts of the Torah there are allusions to this theory; for example, when King David says in Psalms, "Please, God, protect my spirit from the sword, and my soul from the dogs." Rabbi Hayim Vital explains that King David is alluding to the idea of reincarnation. King David is asking God to protect his soul from being reincarnated into a dog. This is the idea of reincarnation from the human species into a lower level of creation, descending into the animal kingdom. Furthermore, according to the teachings of the Holy Ari Zal, there is also the notion of reincarnations of human souls into the level of vegetation and even descending into the level of the inanimate, the inorganic. As the Prophet says, "For a stone from the walls will scream, and a piece of wood from the tree will cry." This verse, says Reb Hayim, is also alluding to the concept of reincarnation: a human soul who is now reincarnated into a stone or a piece of wood and is crying from the pain it suffers, that of being a human soul trapped in the body of a stone.

It is self-explanatory that these verses from the revealed scriptures of the Torah are not actual *proof* of reincarnation, rather, they are hints and allusions. In truth, we do not need any proof of reincarnation, from the Niglah of Torah. The very name, Kabbalah, means "receiving," thus implying that the Kabbalah was received from one generation to the next, going back until the giving of the Torah on Mount Sinai, some 3,300 years ago at which time God gave and revealed to man the mundane, as well as the mystical, elements of the Torah. And there, God revealed to man all the hidden insights of the Torah including an essential teaching of the Kabbalah, the concept of reincarna-

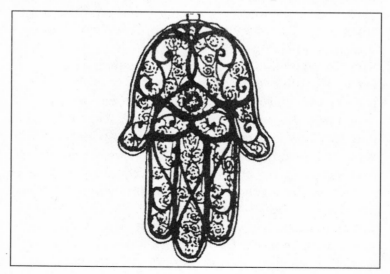

tion, of which there is no disagreement in terms of its validity in the kabbalistic traditions.

Reincarnation was considered to be a well-established fact throughout our history. Especially in the traditions of the Kabbalah. It was known in all the

---

*Reincarnation was considered to be a
well-established fact throughout our history.*

---

secret societies to the groups of people who would study the esoteric together. Josephus (the famous Jewish historian, 37-93 c.e.) writes of an accepted belief by many religious Jews — the concept of reincarnation. To quote, "Do ye not remember at all pure spirits who are in conformity with the divine . . . and in the course of time they are again sent down to inhabit sinless bodies." Moreover, even amongst the gentiles, this concept was well known. Many of the ancient Greek philosophers, who preceded Aristotle, believed in the idea of reincarnation.

For example, the Greek philosopher and mathematician Pythagoras (582-507 b.c.e.) would speak of the previous lives that he led before he descended into the body of Pythagoras. The greatest of the Greek philosophers, Plato (427-347 b.c.e.), writes not only of the concept of reincarnation of souls between one human being and the next, but he also writes of transmigration of souls from humans into the animal kingdom.

However, these mystical concepts of Kabbalah were not common knowledge, taught to any student who came to study at the talmudic academies. In fact, the Kabbalah was usually not taught in these academies at all, rather, it was given over from one person to the next, from one generation to the next in secret, studied only in certain secret societies of Kabbalists. Therefore, it is understood that even amongst many of the great talmudic scholars and rabbis throughout the generations, these teachings were not studied, or even heard of. There were some great Jewish thinkers who

---

*Even amongst many of the great talmudic scholars
and rabbis throughout the generations, these
teachings were not studied, or even heard of.*

---

claimed that this notion of reincarnation is not a Jewish idea at all. (Even though many of the leaders of Israel did not receive this Kabbalah and argued that it is indeed a Jewish concept.) The sages who did not receive this Kabbalah from their teachers argued against reincarnation using logical arguments. But we have already established that the reason we do believe in reincarnation is not because we have found good reason for it, rather, because that is what God revealed to us in the Kabbalah, whose source goes back to Mount Sinai. Hence, any logical argument for or against this concept has no validity, because it is not with our intelligence or our own intuition that we established this belief, it is by revelation.

From *Reincarnation and Judaism: The Journey of the Soul.*

Rabbi DovBer Pinson was born and raised in Brooklyn, New York. He attended the Yeshiva Oholei Torah and went on to study in the Yeshiva Toras Emes in Jerusalem where he received his *semicha* from prominent rabbis and *poskim*. He returned to the States where he began to travel on behalf of Chabad outreach programs. He served as rabbi for the Jewish community in Kobe, Japan and still returns there to visit occasionally. Rabbi Pinson is currently studying in Kolel. He lectures and writes on Jewish mysticism, philosophy, and history.

18

The Sabbath
and the Kabbalah

David S. Ariel

Most modern Sabbath observers are unaware of the extent to which Jewish mystics, particularly the Kabbalists of Safed in the sixteenth century, introduced into Jewish practice new rituals that reflected their mystical view of the Sabbath. For example, it was their custom to go out into the fields to greet the Sabbath. They went out dressed in white ready to join the bride as her entourage in the wedding ceremony. They would face the west from where the *Shekhinah* would rise as the sun set. The order of prayers for the Friday evening service that accompanied this ritual was established by these mystics as a unitive and restorative ritual. Their order, including the mystical hymn *Lekhah Dodi,* which was discussed above, prevails even today.

The *Zohar* included certain blessings such as "who extends a tent of peace" (*ha-pores sukkat shalom*) and excluded certain prayers such as "He is merciful and acquits transgression" (*ve-hu rahum yikhapper avvon*) from the Friday evening service, to illustrate the notion that unity prevails and severity is annulled on the Sabbath.

The elaborate Friday evening service is not the only mystical Sabbath rite that entered normative practice. The *Zohar* explains that the head of the household must accomplish ten things at the Sabbath table, corresponding to the ten *Sefirot*. Although many of these are rabbinic practices, the enumeration of ten central customs and the associated symbolism are Zoharic:

1. Light at least two Sabbath candles: The woman head of the household lights at least two Sabbath

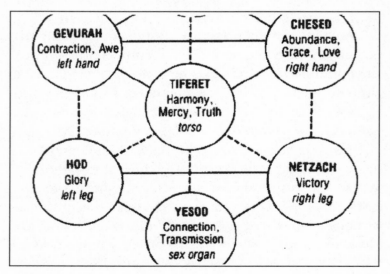

candles at the table before the onset of the Sabbath, corresponding to the two versions of the Sabbath law in the Decalogue. In the *Zohar* the candles symbolize *Hesed* (mercy), and the table symbolizes *Din* (severity). Symbolically, this act dispels *Din* from the table.

2. Bless the cup of wine: The male recites the *Kiddush,* the Sabbath blessing, over wine at the table. The first part of the *Kiddush,* taken from the biblical description of the first Sabbath, is associated with *Yesod,* a masculine *Sefirah.* The second section is associated with the feminine *Malkhut.* Together, the *Kiddush* symbolizes the unification of masculine and feminine *Sefirot.*

3. Perform the ritual handwashing before breaking bread: This rabbinic law is a requirement before eating bread. The *Zohar* requires that one hold a cup filled with water in the right hand, which symbolizes *Hesed,* pass the cup to the left hand, which symbolizes *Din,* and pour it first upon the right hand then pass the cup again and pour upon the left. This is done so that the priority of *Hesed* over *Din* on the Sabbath is emphasized.

4. Put two loaves of bread on the table: Two loaves are traditionally used to recall the double portion of manna that rained down on the Sabbath. According to the *Zohar* the two loaves placed together symbolize the union of *Malkhut* and *Tiferet.* The *Zohar* requires that the diners eat from the lower of the two loaves,

160   *3-Minute Discourses*

when one is placed on top of the other, to symbolize the lower *Sefirot,* especially *Malkhut.*

5. Eat three festive meals: The major meals of the Sabbath are Friday evening, Saturday lunch, and later on Saturday following the late afternoon service. According to the *Zohar* these meals ceremoniously invoke the power of *Malkhut, Keter,* and *Tiferet,* respectively. Special songs (*zemirot*) are sung at each of the meals, many of which were composed as hymns to the *Sefirah* associated with that meal.

6. Discuss Torah at the table: According to the rabbinic tradition, the *Shekhinah* dwells at any table where Torah is discussed.

7. Welcome poor guests to the table: Charitable concern for the poor is a feature of the social consciousness of the *Zohar.* The poor are believed to bring special merit to the table and aid in the achievement of unity.

8. Perform ritual handwashing after the meal: This is a rabbinic custom called *final water* (*mayyin aharonim*). It is done after the meal before saying the blessing after food. The *Zohar* explains that this custom is performed in order to cleanse the hands of evil and to remove the impurities that cling to them. It is also intended to wash away particles of food which are then considered a concession and nournishment to the evil forces.

9. Recite the blessing after food: This rabbinic practice is associated, according to the *Zohar*, with the *Sefirah Hesed*. The *Zohar* explains that one who says this blessing with intention will invoke *Hased* upon the world.

10. Bless a final cup of wine: According to rabbinic tradition a final cup of wine is blessed following the blessing after food.

These practices illustrate the way Jewish mystics reinterpret traditional practices in light of mystical teachings. The Sabbath is turned into a theurgic drama that unfolds in sequence.

The mystics also introduced completely new customs. For example, the custom of singing *Eshet Hayyil* ("Woman of Valor") as a hymn at the Sabbath table in praise of the wife and alluding to the *Shekhinah* was introduced by the Safed Kabbalists.

Ritual innovation can also be seen in the *Zohar*'s approach to human sexuality. The *Zohar* considers Sabbath the most propitious occasion for unitive and restorative mysticism through human sexual intercourse.

The Zohar *considers Sabbath the most propitious occasion for unitive and restorative mysticism through human sexual intercourse.*

Sexual intercourse on Sabbath eve produces the special Sabbath soul. Therefore, this is the time when a righteous man and woman should have sexual contact. The themes of mystical reinterpretation and innovation can be seen in regard to other Jewish rituals.

From *The Mystic Quest: An Introduction to Jewish Mysticism.*

David S. Ariel, former assistant professor of religion at Wesleyan University in Connecticut, is currently president of the Cleveland College of Jewish Studies. He has taught Judaica at Boston University and Hebrew at Brandeis University, where he received his Ph.D. in Jewish philosophy and *Kabbalah*. He has taught and lectured in the United States, Israel, and the Soviet Union, and has published articles on Jewish and Islamic mysticism in the *Brown University Judaica Series, Judaism, Religious Studies Review,* and *New Outlook.*

19

The Reason for Creation in Kabbalistic Thought

Chaim Dalfin

An important term to understand is *dirah bitacht-onim,* which means making a dwelling place, a house for God on earth, just as a person has a home. The Midrash says that God had a desire to have a home and He desired to have His home here, not anywhere else. This is elucidated in the *Tanya* on the basis of a saying found in the *Midrash Tanchuman.* The Alter Rebbe (the first Lubavitcher Rebbe) explains that *nisaveh haKodesh Boruch Hu lihyos lo dirah bitach-tonim,* meaning God desired to have an abode on earth, refers specifically to this mundane and corporeal world. He explains that the higher worlds discussed in Kabbalah are all spiritual. They are worlds of revelation, but the essence of God cannot be grasped through spiritual revelation. It will be shown that this material world, as a place of spiritual darkness, is the place where God's essence can dwell.

The word *nisaveb* in this context needs interpretation. The normal word used in the Hebrew language meaning "want" is *ratzah*. Therefore, when describing God's desire for creation, seemingly the more appropriate word might be *"ratzah HaKodesh Boruch. . . ."* Chasidus explains that the choice of the word *nisaveh* and not *ratzah* not only communicates the purpose of creation, which is the what in creation, but also the who involved in creation.

To understand this, it will help to mention some reasons for creation. In the Kabbalah there are several reasons mentioned why God created the world. One reason is that, since God's nature is good, therefore it is natural for the good to do good. For example, a person

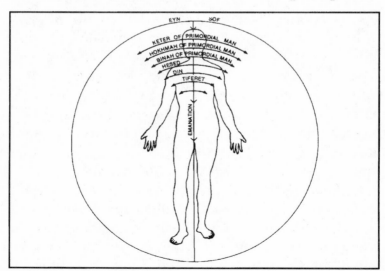

who is truly good won't be able to function unless he or she is performing acts of loving-kindness. This type of an individual will seek out others to help. Following this logic, God, being naturally good, seeks something to bestow His goodness upon. Hence He made the mundane world. Chasidus doesn't accept this as a final reason for creation, because God transcends nature, God acts in supernatural ways when He so desires. So to say God's nature is good is a limitation on God's true infinity. Just as in the example, a person who is compelled by his nature, even though he does great benevolent acts, yet this very virtue of character limits

---

In the Kabbalah there are several reasons mentioned why God created the world.

---

him to always being good. There are times when this same person needs to be strict and severe, and yet he isn't able to free himself from his "good" nature. In contemporary terms, he can't say no. The same follows regarding God. To say God's nature is good is tantamount to saying God is limited and forced to act in a certain way, and that simply isn't true. When He so desires, God manifests Himself in what we call good, and when He desires to act in a manner that we perceive as strict, that is His choice. It is for this reason that Chasidus rejects this explanation as the ultimate purpose for creation. God could just as easily have created the world in such a way that His action would be based on His supernatural qualities, which aren't necessarily limited to projecting goodness in the format adapted to our way of life and understanding of the universe.

Another reason mentioned in the Kabbalah for creation is that God wanted someone to appreciate His creation. Therefore, He created the physical mundane world with people being the subjects. Again here Chasidus doesn't accept this as the *ultimate* reason for creation because the heavenly realms that were created appreciate His greatness much more than we do. This world is full of *klipah* — negative energy — and the wicked prosper. Here a human must struggle to appreciate God and face many tests on a daily basis just to control human passions. So why would God in His infinite wisdom create a world that conceals Him? This refutation is alluded to in the section of the Tanya mentioned earlier. The Alter Rebbe says that since these spiritual worlds are a descent and digression in comparison to God's essence, they aren't the ultimate reason for creation. I heard another way of explaining these words. Since there are always other lower worlds below those spiritual realms, the spiritual realms aren't the ultimate reason for creation, otherwise why did God create something "lower and more coarse than the spiritual refined levels? Based on this interpretation, the meaning of "since they are a descent" means that there is a descent and something even lower. If this is the case, it is obvious that God desired something lower, and in fact He desired the lowest of the low! Therefore Chasidus says that God's desire to have someone to appreciate His creation is not the ultimate reason. So what is the ultimate reason for creation?

The answer is, there is no answer. To understand this requires focus on the exact language used in the Midrash Tanchumah. The word *nisaveh* comes from

---

*So what is the ultimate reason for creation? The
answer is, there is no answer.*

---

the Hebrew word *taivah,* meaning a desire beyond
rational. In modern culture it would be called a lust.
The word *lust* has a negative connotation. However,
the Hebrew word *taivah,* means a strong desire that
impacts the person in such a way that nothing else
does. Simply put, when a person has a *taivah* for a
certain thing, he doesn't use his rational power of
judgment at all. If something smells or tastes good, he
wants it. The same is true in regard to God creating the
world. God had a *taivah* to create the world. He didn't
allow anything to get in His way, including those rational reasons mentioned earlier. Therefore, when the
question is asked, "why did He need this materialistic
world?" the answer is, God had a positive spiritual lust!
As the Alter Rebbe put it, *"Uf a taivah, iz nit kein
kashah"*: When you have a spiritual lust, there's no
question. Desire transcends questioning.

   The Alter Rebbe explained as follows: *"Uf a taivah,
iz nit kein kashah"*: Regarding a *taivah,* a spiritual
desire, there is no question. Why? Because when we
talk about Hashem's lust to create the world (the word
taivah is used in the Midrash), there is no why. God
creates the why and the answers. It's an oxymoron, a
contradictory expression. If Hashem is omnipotent,
then to say that Hashem has to give an answer is
limiting God to questions and answers — to the realm of
rationality, which God transcends by definition.
Hashem can certainly ask questions and give answers

whenever He wants; but to say that humans must be given a why is limiting, and it contradicts the idea that Hashem can create anything. Such a limited God would not be the God of the Torah. This would be the who involved with creation. Since the reason for creation comes from God, who is beyond human reasoning, therefore the part of God involved in creation is the true absolute essence of God. It is similar to a person who has a particular *taivah*. Stop and ask him where is it coming from, and he won't be able to give you an answer, because the *taivah* comes from a place within the person that transcends questions and answers. It comes from the essence of the individual.

From *Demystifying the Mystical: Understanding the Language and Concepts of Chasidism and Jewish Mysticism*.

Chaim Dalfin received his rabbinical ordination from the Central Yeshiva Tomchei Temimim Lubavitch in Brooklyn, New York. He received his Bachelor of Religious Studies degree from the Rabbinical College of America in Morristown, New Jersey.

20

Kabbalistic
Conceptions of Death

Simcha Paull Raphael

The following observations can be made about the
postmortem conceptions of Kabbalah:

1. According to kabbalistic teachings, each dimension of the multileveled soul—*nefesh*, *ruah*,
   neshamah, *hayyah*, *yehidah*—goes through
   different experiences on the afterlife journey.
   The lower levels of the soul are purified and
   purged of physical and emotional attachments,
   while the higher levels experience transcendental bliss.
2. Kabbalistic teachings demonstrate an acute
   understanding of the dying process itself. The
   Zohar and other mystical texts describe death-

bed visions, the postmortem life review and
judgment, and the painful separation of body
from soul/spirit.

3. Within the kabbalistic tradition Gehenna is conceived of as a purification process in which
psychic remnants from the previous life are
purged and transformed. This purgation process
lasts only twelve months and is tormentingly
painful in direct proportion to each individual's
lived life experience.

4. For the kabbalists, Gan Eden is conceived of in a
dual sense. Lower Gan Eden is the realm in
which one experiences the bliss of the higher
emotions; Upper Gan Eden is yet a more transcendental realm in which one realizes the re-
sults of one's lofty, spiritual thoughts of the
previous life and communes directly with God.

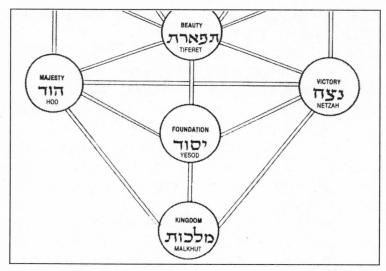

5. *Gilgul*, the doctrine of reincarnation, became increasingly important in kabbalistic Judaism from the twelfth century onward. For the kabbalists, the process of physical reembodiment made it possible for one to fulfill all the *mitzvot*, or commandments.

Kabbalistic teachings demonstrate an acute understanding of the dying process itself.

---

6. At the folk level, *gilful* led to the development of an extensive literary tradition on possession by reincarnating spirits. The terms used in this context were *dybbukkim*, spirits of malevolent possession, and *ibburrim*, souls of benevolent possession.

7. The kabbalists reaffirmed the rabbinic belief in resurrection of the dead. However, they added a spiritual context to this doctrine, understanding the resurrection as being a materialization of the fully awakened spiritual body.

8. In kabbalistic writings, a psychological orientation to the postmortem journey is evident. Although the rabbinic doctrine of divine retribution underlies kabbalistic eschatology, the kabbalists made a significant contribution to Jewish afterlife tradition by developing a; more psychologically oriented description of the after-death experiences. The afterlife teachings of the kabbalists are couched more in a psychological tone than uniquely in an ethical one. Gan Eden and Gehenna are not simply regions of reward or

punishment; they are postmortem spiritual states of awareness that mirror the quality of one's emotional and mental consciousness while alive in the physical body.

From *Jewish Views of the Afterlife.*

Simcha Paull Raphael received a doctorate in psychology from the California Institute of Integral Studies in San Francisco and ordination as a rabbinic pastor from Rabbi Zalman Schachter-Shalomi. He is currently an assistant professor in the Department of Religion and Jewish chaplain at LaSalle University. Dr. Raphael is also in private practice as a psychotherapist specializing in bereavement. Originally from Montreal, he and his wife, Geela Rayzel, now reside in Philadelphia with their son, Yigdal.

21

The Paradox of Nothingness in Kabbalah

Joseph Dan

In the early thirteenth century, *ayin*, the Hebrew word for "nothingness," became one of the most important and profound symbols of the Kabbalah. It appears in the works of the early kabbalists in Provence and in Spain, especially in the treatises written by a Jewish mystical group in the small town of Gerona in Catalonia. Later, this concept was extensively used by Rabbi Moses de Leon, the author of the *Zohar*, the greatest and most influential text of the Kabbalah written in northern Spain in the end of the thirteenth century. The *Zohar*'s understanding of symbols became central for later Jewish mystics, including the teachers of Hasidism in the eighteenth and nineteenth centuries.

Most kabbalistic symbols were derived directly from the Bible. Every biblical verse was interpreted by kabbalists in a mystical way, and key words and terms found in them became standard kabbalistic symbols. The history of the term *ayin*, however, is unique. This term was based on a philosophical cosmogonic concept, which the kabbalists adopted, integrated into a biblical verse, and gave a completely new and paradoxical meaning.

When Jewish philosophers in the tenth to twelfth centuries endeavored to harmonize the text of the scriptures describing the creation of the world with the teachings of the Greek classical philosophers concerning the origin of the world, one of the key terms they had to use was creation *ex nihilo*, "out of nothingness," as opposed to creation from primordial matter or the Aristotelian concept of eternal, non-created world. The

term they adopted (in the Hebrew works of Rabbi
Solomon ibn Gabirol, Rabbi Abraham bar Hijja, Rabbi
Abraham ibn Ezra, and others) was creation *yesh me-
ayin*, "something out of nothing," thus giving the Hebrew biblical term *ayin* the meaning of complete
negation, absolute nothingness. Although they did not
mean to do it, they gave this Hebrew word the associa-
tion of being the first, most ancient, and most fundamental stage in the process of creation. *Ayin* thus
became a term loaded with mysterious connotations
that enabled the mystics to use it in a completely
different manner.

---

*Every biblical verse was interpreted by kabbalists
in a mystical way, and key words and terms
found in them became standard kabbalistic
symbols.*

Another text that contributed to the mysterious
character of this term was a cryptic passage in the *Sefer
Yezirah* (Book of Creation), an ancient cosmogonical
work, which probably was written in the fourth century by a Jewish mystic-scientist who used terminology
characteristic only of this text. The *Sefer Yezirah* had
an enormous influence on the medieval Jewish kabbalists; all of its terms and phrases were closely studied
and often used. In the sixth paragraph of the second
chapter of this brief work we read: "He (God) created
from *tohu* (chaos) — substance, and made *eino ye-
shno.*" This phrase can be interpreted as either "He
made from what is not what is," or "He made from His
nothingness His substance." The term *eino* can be
interpreted as referring to some divine attribute, some-

thing that is not just nothingness, but a kind of attribute within the precreation of divine existence.

When the Kabbalah emerged in Provence and northern Spain in the last years of the twelfth century and at the beginning of the thirteenth, a new element was added to the Jewish conception of the Godhead: the idea that there are ten divine powers, hypostases of

---

The process of creation in the Kabbalah is first and foremost the story of the process of emanation of these ten powers, called sefirot.

---

the supreme divine being, which are emanated one from the other. The process of creation in the Kabbalah is first and foremost the story of the process of emanation of these ten powers, called *sefirot* (a term also derived from the *Sefer Yezirah*). These ten *sefirot* are the main subject of kabbalistic speculation. In the thirteenth century, the term *ayin* became the appellation of the first and highest divine power, the source of all divine and material existence.

The early kabbalists who used this term relied consistently on one verse, Job 28:12, which reads: "But wisdom, where shall it be found? And where is the place of understanding?" The medieval Jewish mystics found in this verse a description of the emanation of the first three divine powers. According to them, the second *sefirah* is called *chochmath*, wisdom, and the third is called *binah*, understanding. They disregarded the phrasing of the verse as a question, and read it as a statement. Yet as a statement the Hebrew text does not imply a wondering as to where is a place or source of wisdom, but a divine exclamation that the origin of wisdom is in the *ayin* (the Hebrew *me-ayin* can be read both as a question, "Wherefrom?" and as a statement: from the *ayin*, from nothingness). For them, this verse therefore meant that God Himself declared the origin of the second and third divine nypostases to be the first, which he called *ayin*.

This terminology, found, for instance, in Rabbi Azriel of Gerona's commentary on the talmudic legends (I. Tishby's edition, Jerusalem 1945, pp. 90 and 107), transformed the meaning of the philosophical term "nothingness" to the highest and most divine form of existence. Thus a term that was used to denote negation and nonexistence was transformed to mean the first spiritual step that creates a bridge between the completely hidden and inactive Godhead and the emanated divine *sefirot*. Within the realm of this *ayin*, the divine will to create, to form something outside of itself, is being expressed. On the one hand, therefore, the *ayin* is still a symbol of nothingness, because when it was emanated nothing was as yet in actual existence. All that this symbol represents is the first spark of divine will or thought to emanate divine beings of positive existence. On the other hand, this term denotes existence in its most supreme sense. The kabbalists followed in many respects neo-Platonist ideas, and the closer a being is to the divine source, the truer is its existence. The *ayin*, in this sense, exists in a truer manner than everything which is below it, which was emanated from it.

~

It should be noted that the early kabbalists did not use the same term when they referred to the highest

divine realm, the Godhead itself, which is beyond any
description, even a symbolic one, and which is eternal
and unchanging; they called this realm *ein sof*, meaning "no end." This is a completely negative term that
does not convey any specific meaning; any other negative term could be, and sometimes was, used in its
place, because *ein sof* refers to the divine realm in
which no positive linguistic terms can apply, and therefore all negatives are equally relevant. The *ayin*, the
highest *sefirah*, often described by the symbol *keter*
(crown), is therefore the first positive divine symbol
emerging from the negatively described *ein sof*. The
Zohar, the most important kabbalistic work of the
Middle Ages, even strengthens the paradoxical relationship between *ayin* and *ein sof* by stating: "*Ein sof*
cannot be known, it makes neither end nor beginning,
but the primordial *ayin* emanated beginning and end"
(Zohar vol. II, p. 239b). The author emphasizes here
that while the term "end" has no meaning when applied to *ein sof*, it does have a meaning when applied to
ayin, the first and highest emanation from *ein sof*.

Various kabbalists used this symbolism in different
ways, and in the history of the Kabbalah no consistency
can be found in the detailed use of this terminology.
The paradoxical nature of the *ayin*, however, remained
constant in almost all medieval mystical speculations,
and was integrated, especially in the *Zohar*, within a
system of similar paradoxes: Darkness is the supreme
light, silence is the supreme sound, and other similar
statements. Still, the close relationship between the
symbols of existence and nonexistence was used by
many mystics as a source for profound speculations
and vivid paradoxical descriptions. The relationship

*Darkness is the supreme light, silence is the
supreme sound.*

between the first *sefirah* and the Godhead itself was
always one of the most intriguing subjects of mystical
inquiry, and the problem of the eternity of the *ayin* and
its relationship to the *ein sof* have often been discussed. Even the *Zohar* itself contains more than one
view on this subject.

The paradoxical nature of the term "nothingness"
in the Kabbalah opened a space for speculations and
even had a strong impact on actual religious life, as it
became apparent centuries later. Kabbalists followed
the philosophers and spoke of a creation *ex nihilo*,
although they gave these terms an entirely different
meaning. This did not mean the creation of something
out of nothing, but the emergence of all existence from
the supreme source of existence that is the divine
ayin. They spoke of the emergence of all existence
from its hidden root within the Godhead; for them
existence and nonexistence became one and the
same in that hidden realm their source, where, as they
sometimes said, all the contradictions are united. For
these kabbalists, the mystical secret of being and nonbeing became united in the profound and powerful
symbol of the *ayin*.

Mystical activity in the Kabbalah was used to uplift
the human soul from its material surroundings and
unite it with the divine powers. The ladder of emanation, leading from the first to the tenth *sefirah*, and
then to the material world, was used as a ladder of

ascension. Speculation concerning the emergence of the divine hypostases from the Godhead became also a series of directions concerning the way that the mystic's soul has to take in its attempt to ascend and unite itself with the divine realm. Thus, the *ayin*, the first and highest divine emanation, became also the supreme goal of mystical ascension.

The paradox, therefore, acquired a new strength when the unity with nothingness became the supreme achievement of the mystical way toward the mystical union. In most cases kabbalists did not believe that such a union is possible while a man is alive in the material world. With few exceptions, most of them held that the highest stages of communion with the divine powers may occur only after the body's death. Nevertheless, the powerful symbol of a union with "nothingness" did not lose its literal meaning, as it became apparent especially in the last development stages of the mystical schools within Judaism—the Hasidic movement of the second half of the eighteenth century.

Hasidic teachings are based completely on kabbalistic symbolism, but very often the teachers of this

---

Hasidic teachings are based completely on kabbalistic symbolism.

---

modern movement found new meanings in the old symbols and applied them to actual religious life. Hasidism, unlike kabbalism in general, was a popular movement that tried to influence the Jewish public as a whole, and the number of its adherents reached hundreds of thousands and even millions. When paradoxical symbols are transformed into popular teachings for the masses, changes are bound to occur.

In Hasidic teachings we find the term *ayin* in contexts that seem to denote simply its old meaning: nothingness. The faithful are instructed to devote their religious energies to self-negation in a spiritual sense, emptying themselves of all thoughts and feelings of the material world and "becoming nothingness," thus making themselves into vehicles for the pure flow of divine emanation. In some Hasidic schools, the slogan "turning into nothingness" acquired a central place in the teachings concerning one's attitude during prayer and worship. It is obvious, however, that the whole history of this term and its development through eight centuries of mystical speculation is hidden within these seemingly simplistic religious instructions.

"Becoming nothing" is a religious goal because nothingness is the essential attribute of the divine. This is so only because the paradox "Nothingness is the true existence" has been retained and even strengthened.

"Becoming nothing" is a religious goal because nothingness is the essential attribute of the divine.

The denial of the false existence, that is, material existence, is achieved by the unity with nothingness, that is, the supreme divine existence. When becoming "nothing" in comparison to this world, the Hasid achieve "something" in the true, divine world, where true existence (that is, of nothingness) can be found. In Hasidic teaching there are different shades of literal and symbolic meaning of this subject, but in most cases the identity between nothingness and supreme divine existence has been retained and even strengthened.

The popularity of Hasidism, both within Judaism and in modern descriptions of Jewish mysticism, made the paradoxical meaning of *ayin* well known even among non-orthodox and assimilated Jews. Every Jew who lived in the vicinity of a Hasidic community could be exposed to this idea. Such communities were found, in the period before the Second World War, in almost every town in which Jews lived. After the war, nostalgic descriptions of the destroyed Jewish world often have described Hasidic teachings, and some of them emphasize this element. The studies of Hasidism by Martin Buber and Gershom Scholem invariably dwelled on it. A Jewish intellectual in Europe could hardly escape being aware of it. To what extent Paul Celan was influenced by it is, therefore, a meaningful question to be studied.

From *Jewish Mysticism: The Modern Period.*

Professor Joseph Dan is the Gershom Scholem Professor of Kabbalah at Hebrew University of Jerusalem. Born in Bratislava, Slovakia in 1935, his parents immigrated to Jerusalem in 1938. He received his B.A. (1956), M.A. (1958), and Ph.D. (1963) from Hebrew University. Professor Dan has served as the Head of the Institute for Jewish Studies in Hebrew University, and as the Director of the Jewish University and National Library. He has also served as a visiting professor at UCLA, UC Berkeley, Brown University, Colombia University, Harvard University, Princeton Institute of Advanced Study, and University College, London. Professor Dan has published over forty books in Hebrew and English. He was the recipient of the 1997 Israel Prize.

Selected Resources

Shlomo Carlebach

The Holy Beggars' Banquet:
Traditional Jewish Tales and Teachings of
the Great Reb Shlomo Carlebach and Others
in the Spirit of the 1960s, the 1970s, and the
New Age *edited by Kalman Serkez*
(0-7657-9995-2) $40.00

Holy Brother: Inspiring Stories and
Enchanted Tales about Rabbi Shlomo
Carlebach *Yitta Halberstam Mandelbaum*
(0-7657-5959-4) $30.00

Shlomo's Stories: Selected Tales
*Shlomo Carlebach, with Susan Yael
Mesinai* (1-56821-215-1) $30.00

Classics in Translation

The Bahir *translated and with a
commentary by Aryeh Kaplan*
(1-56821-383-2) $40.00

Sefer Yetzirah: The Book of Creation
*translated and with a commentary by
Aryeh Kaplan* (1-56821-503-7) $50.00

The Tree of Life, Volume I: The
Palace of Adam Kadmon (Chayyim Vital's
Introduction to the Kabbalah of Isaac Luria)
by Donald Wilder Menzi and Zwe Padeh
(0-7657-6011-8) $50.00

Gematria

Building Blocks of the Soul: Studies
on the Letters and Words of the Hebrew
Language *Matityahu Glazerson*
(1-56821-932-6) $50.00

The Secrets of Hebrew Words
Benjamin Blech (0-87668-610-2) $30.00

More Secrets of Hebrew Words:
Holy Days and Happy Days *Benjamin
Blech* (0-87668-223-9) $30.00

Hasidic Thought

The Candle of God: Discourses on
Chasidic Thought *Adin Steinsaltz*
(0-7657-6065-7) $40.00

In the Beginning: Discourses on
Chasidic Thought *Adin Steinsaltz*
(1-56821-741-2) $30.00 sc

The Sustaining Utterance:
Discourses on Chasidic Thought *Adin
Steinsaltz* (1-56821-997-0) $25.00 sc

**Wisdom, Understanding, and
Knowledge:** Basic Concepts of Hasidic
Thought *Shmuel Boteach* (0-87668-557-2)
$30.00 sc

Kabbalah/Mysticism

The Alef-Beit: Jewish Thought Revealed
through the Hebrew Letters *Yitzchak
Ginsburgh* (1-56821-413-8) $40.00 sc

Demystifying the Mystical:
Understanding the Language and Concepts
of Chasidism and Jewish Mysticism — A
Primer for the Layman *Chaim Dalfin*
(1-56821-453-7) $25.00

**The Fundamentals of Jewish
Mysticism:** The Book of Creation and Its
Commentaries *Leonard R. Glotzer*
(0-87668-437-1) $40.00

**The Inner Meaning of the Hebrew
Letters** *Robert M. Haralick*
(1-56821-356-5) $40.00

**Jewish Mystical Leaders and
Leadership in the Thirteenth
Century** *edited by Moshe Idel and
Mortimer Ostow* (0-7657-5994-2) $40.00 sc

Jewish Mysticism *Joseph Dan*

Volume I—Late Antiquity
(0-7657-6007-X) $50.00

Volume II—The Middle Ages
(0-7657-6008-8) $50.00

Volume III—The Modern Period
(0-7657-6009-6) $50.00

**Volume IV—General
Characteristics and Comparative
Studies** (0-7657-6010-X) $50.00

**Jewish Mysticism and Jewish
Ethics** *Joseph Dan* (1-56821-563-0)
$25.00 sc

Kabbalah: The Splendor of Judaism
David M. Wexelman (0-7657-6108-4)
$30.00

Kabbalistic Metaphors: Jewish
Mystical Themes in Ancient and Modern
Thought *Sanford L. Drob* (0-7657-6125-4)
$30.00

Magic, Mysticism, and Hasidism:
The Supernatural in Jewish Thought
*Gedalyah Nigal, translated by Edward
Levin* (1-56821-033-7) $40.00

The Mystic Quest: An Introduction to
Jewish Mysticism *David S. Ariel*
(0-87668-928-4) $30.00

Reflections on Infinity: Introduction
to Kabbalah *Raoul Nass* (0-7657-6062-2)
$40.00

The Sefirot: Ten Emanations of Divine
Power *Y. David Shulman* (1-56821-929-6)
$40.00

Symbols of the Kabbalah:
Philosophical and Psychological
Perspectives *Sanford L. Drob*
(0-7657-6126-2) $30.00

Meditation

Meditation and Kabbalah *Aryeh
Kaplan* (1-56821-381-6) $50.00

Meditation and the Bible *Aryeh
Kaplan* (1-56821-382-4) $30.00

The Practice of the Kabbalah:
Meditation in Judaism *Steven Fisdel*
(1-56821-508-8) $40.00

Music

Inner Rhythms: The Kabbalah of Music
DovBer Pinson (0-7657-6098-3) $25.00

Reincarnation

**The Jewish Concept of
Reincarnation and Creation:** Based
on the Writings of Chaim Vital *David M.
Dexelman* (0-7657-5998-5) $40.00

Reincarnation and Judaism: The
Journey of the Soul *DovBer Pinson*
(0-7657-6064-9) $30.00

Zalman Schacter-Shalomi

Paradigm Shift: From the Jewish
Renewal Teachings of Reb Zalman
Schacter-Shalomi *Zalman Schacter-Shalomi,
edited by Ellen Singer* (0-7657-6123-8)
$30.00 sc

Sexuality

The Yetzer: A Kabbalistic Psychology of
Eroticism and Human Sexuality *Mordechai
Rotenberg* (1-56821-898-2) $40.00 sc

Adin Steinsaltz

The Candle of God: Discourses on
Chasidic Thought *Adin Steinsaltz*
(0-7657-6065-7) $40.00

In the Beginning: Discourses on
Chasidic Thought *Adin Steinsaltz*
(1-56821-741-2) $30.00

The Long Shorter Way: Discourses
on Chasidic Thought *Adin Steinsaltz*
(1-56821-144-9) $30.00

On Being Free
Adin Steinsaltz
(0-7657-9985-5) $30.00

The Seven Lights: On the Major
Jewish Festivals *Adin Steinsaltz and Josy
Eisenberg* (0-7657-6156-4) $40.00

The Strife of the Spirit
Adin Steinsaltz (1-56821-981-4) $30.00

The Sustaining Utterance:
Discourses on Chasidic Thought
Adin Steinsaltz (1-56821-997-0) $25.00

The Thirteen Petalled Rose
Adin Steinstalz (0-87668-450-9) $30.00

The Tales of Rabbi Nachman of Bratslav *retold with commentary by Adin Steinsaltz* (0-87668-183-6) $35.00

Appendix

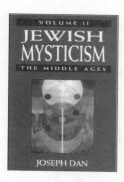

JEWISH MYSTICISM
Volume I—Late Antiquity
0-7657-6007-X, $50.00

Volume II—The Middle Ages
0-7657-6008-8, $50.00

Volume III—The Modern Period
0-7657-6009-6, $50.00

Volume IV—
General Characteristics and
Comparative Studies
0-7657-6010-X, $50.00
Joseph Dan

This four-volume work is a monumental event in the publishing history of English-language reference books on the subject of Jewish mystical thought and practice. Professor Dan's credentials are of the highest order. The recipient of the Israel Prize (considered to be Israel's highest honor), Joseph Dan is the Gershom Scholem Professor of Kabbalah at the Hebrew University of Jerusalem, and continues to be a visiting professor at some of the most prestigious institutions of higher learning in the world.

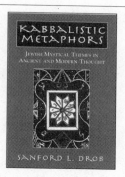

KABBALISTIC METAPHORS:
Jewish Mystical Themes in Ancient
and Modern Thought
Sanford L. Drob
0-7657-6125-4, $30.00
Kabbalistic Metaphors: Jewish Mystical Themes in Ancient and Modern Thought places the major symbols of the theosophical Kabbalah into a dialogue with several systems of ancient and modern thought, including Indian philosophy, Platonism, Gnosticism, and the works of Hegel, Freud, and Jung. The author shows how the Kabbalah organizes a series of ancient ideas regarding God, cosmos, and humanity into a basic metaphor that itself reappears in various guises in much of modern philosophy and psychology. Recognition of the parallels between the Kabbalah and modern philosophy and psychology provides us with valuable insight into both the Kabbalah and modern thought, and helps pave the way for

a "new Kabbalah," one that is spiritually and intellectually relevant to contemporary man.

ON BEING FREE
Adin Steinsaltz
1-56821-321-1, $30.00

On Being Free is a collection of illuminating essays written by one of the leading rabbis of the twentieth century.

In this new volume Rabbi Adin Steinsaltz explores such topics as the fate of the Jewish people, the causes of assimilation, sin and atonement, and mysticism. He also devotes a section of the book to a study of the five *Megillot* of the Bible, drawing out the messages these *Megillot* contain for the modern Jew.

On Being Free serves as an important forum for one of the great Jewish teachers of our time.

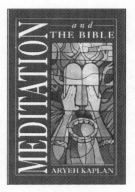

MEDITATION AND THE BIBLE
Aryeh Kaplan
1-56821-382-4, $30.00

One of the greatest mysteries of the Bible involves the methods used by the prophets to attain their unique states of consciousness. Almost all of the Bible was authored by these prophets while in such higher states, but virtually nothing is known about how they were attained. In the actual text of the Bible, very little is said about the methods, and the few relevant passages that do exist are difficult to understand and require adequate interpretation. But unless their methods are known, it is difficult to put the teachings of the prophets of the Bible in their proper context, and consequently, many other concepts found in this sacred book are apt to be understood inadequately.

An important task of this book, therefore, will be to relearn the vocabulary used in classical Hebraic literature to describe the various meditative methods.

For more information: www.aronson.com

DEMYSTIFYING THE MYSTICAL:
Understanding the Language
and Concepts of Chasidism and
Jewish Mysticism—A Primer
for the Layman
Chaim Dalfin
1-56821-453-7, $25.00

Demystifying the Mystical is a primer designed to ease the layperson into the esoteric world of Chasidism.

The concepts found in Jewish mysticism can often be difficult even for the learned person to grasp because its principles are embedded in parables, analogies, and examples. Whether one has had a rich Jewish education or has just been introduced to the world of Jewish thought, the lofty concepts of Kabbalah can be difficult to relate to in a down-to-earth way. "Just as one must master his or her profession in order to succeed, one must learn Chasidism so as to internalize its teachings," says author Rabbi Chaim Dalfin.

Only then do the esoteric principles of mysticism appear in their practical application to today's world.

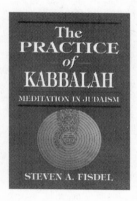

THE PRACTICE OF KABBALAH:
Meditation in Judaism
Steven Fisdel
1-56821-508-8, $40.00

The Practice of Kabbalah: Meditation in Judaism emphasizes meditation within Judaism as the practical core of Jewish mysticism. In this volume, Rabbi Steven Fisdel explores Jewish meditation practices as the experiential side of Kabbalah and therefore as one of the primary sources for the development of the mystic thought and belief in Judaism.

**THE SEFIROT: Ten Emanations of
Divine Power**
Y. David Shulman
1-56821-929-6, $40.00

The Jewish mystical tradition teaches that in order to create the many planes of being that culminated in our world, God brought into being ten *sefirot*, or vessels. These *sefirot* consecutively filtered (and continue to filter) God's spiritual light, so that universes separate from Him were able to emerge. In this book, the author bases his exploration of the ten *sefirot* on the teachings of Rabbi Nachman of Bratslav.

THE BAHIR
*translated and with a commentary
by Aryeh Kaplan*
1-56821-503-7, $50.00

The Bahir is one of the oldest and most important of all classical Kabbalah texts. Until the publication of the Zohar, the Bahir was the most influential and widely quoted primary source of Kabbalistic teachings. It is quoted in every major book on Kabbalah, the earliest being the Raavad's commentary on *Sefer Yetzirah*, and it is cited numerous times by Rabbi Moshe ben Nachman (Ramban) in his commentary on the Torah. It is also quoted many times in the Zohar. It was first published about 1176 by the Provence school of Kabbalists; the first printed edition appeared in Amsterdam in 1651.

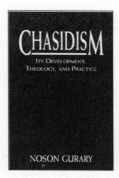

CHASIDISM: Its Development, Theology, and Practice
Noson Gurary
0-7657-5960-8, $00.00

The author writes: "The major aim of this study . . . is to clarify some of the most important axioms of chasidic mystical theology. . . . [Also,] to show that the existential and cosmological views maintained by Chasidism do not contradict human experience or the religious values of normative Judaism, as expressed in the Halachic [legal] codes. On the contrary, Chasidism demands their ultimate synthesis and actualization in daily life."

THE SUSTAINING UTTERANCE: Discourses on Chasidic Thought
Adin Steinsaltz
1-56821-997-0, $25.00

A select group of students who gathered in the basement of a Jerusalem synagogue was privileged to hear the renowned scholar Rabbi Adin Steinsaltz give a series of discourses on Chasidic thought. Faithful to the Chasidic tradition of creating books based on oral teachings, Yehuda Hanegbi has edited and translated these discourses to form *The Sustaining Utterance*, a major exploration of Chasidism.

Like its companion volume, *The Long Shorter Way, The Sustaining Utterance* is a commentary on the *Tanya*, a classic Chasidic work by Rabbi Schneur Zalman of Liadi. Based on the second part of the *Tanya* (entitled "The Gate of Unity and Faith" and also known as "The Education of a Child"), *The*

Sustaining Utterance examines basic theological issues, such as our knowledge of God and of our world.

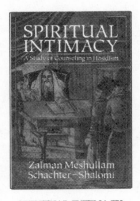

SPIRITUAL INTIMACY:
A Study of Counseling in Hasidism
Zalman Schachter-Shalomi
1-56821-923-7, $35.00

How does one become a rebbe (hasidic master) or a hasid (his disciple)? What is the nature of the relationship between them? What happens during the private interview (known as a *yehidut*) between rebbe and hasid? How does the yehidut compare to other forms of psychological counseling and in what ways is it distinctive? In *Spiritual Intimacy: A Study of Counseling in Hasidism*, Zalman Schachter-Shalomi provides a thorough exploration of these issues.

The author discusses how one becomes a rebbe and the personality types best suited to it. The author examines the various stages in the training of a prospective rebbe, the tests he must undergo to prove and strengthen his vocation, and the "gifts of the spirit" with which he is endowed and which aid him in functioning as a rebbe.

THE TREE OF LIFE, Volume I:
The Palace of Adam Kadmon
(Chayyim Vital's Introduction to
the Kabbalah of Isaac Luria)
Donald Wilder Memzi
and Zwe Padeh
0-7657-6011-8, $50.00

Etz Chayyim (The Tree of Life), Chayyim Vital's summary of the teachings of his master, Isaac Luria, is one of the most important books in the history of Kabbalah, the mystical strand of Jewish tradition. Luria himself is generally acknowledged to be the most influential kabbalist, second only to the author of the Zohar, and *Etz Chayyim* is considered by kabbalists and scholars alike to be the most authoritative version of his teachings. This book is the first translation into English of a major portion of this classic work.

This volume — "The Palace of Adam Kadmon" — presents an overview of Isaac Luria's teachings, outlining the entire Lurianic system and providing a detailed description of its main structural elements. This translation of "The Palace of Adam Kadmon" will open this fascinating and important text to a large and growing body of readers who are becoming interested in Kabbalah and are curious about its original sources.

mysical cosmology is described poetically and meditatively. The range of subjects includes the revelation of light within the world and its relationship to human lifecycle and biological processes, including kissing, lovemaking, conception, gestation, birth, nursing, and maturation states.

Eliahu Klein's translation is a groundbreaking effort, as the entire text has been reformatted in poetic style, so the reader can actually enter the text and get a taste of how Isaac Luria actually communicated and transmitted his treachings for the first time to his students.

KABBALAH OF CREATION
Eliahu Klein
0-7657-6130-0, $40.00
Kabbalah of Creation is a breakthrough translation of the early Kabbalah of Rabbi Isaac Luria, the founder of the most influential Jewish mystical school of the last four hundred years. In this volume, a

THE MYSTIC QUEST: An Introduction to Jewish Mysticism
David S. Ariel
0-87668-928-4, $30.00
The Mystic Quest explains the major ideas and concepts of Jewish mystical thought in a way that the general reader can clearly understand.

Drawing upon his own extensive research as well as on the growing body of scholarly material on the subject, Dr. David Ariel, president of the Cleveland College of Jewish Studies, presents the extremely difficult and complex elements of Jewish mysticism in language that makes it accessible to the layperson.

The Mystic Quest begins with an examination of the variety of phenomena known in different cultures as "mysticism." Ariel then locates the Jewish mystical tradition within the context of Jewish history and traces its evolution throughout the ages. Jewish mystical theories about the hidden and revealed God, the feminine aspects of divinity, the mystical Torah, and the concepts of the soul and human destiny are then explored in detail. Finally, the author considers Hasidism and modern Jewish mystical thought, discussing the role of mysticism in contemporary Judaism.

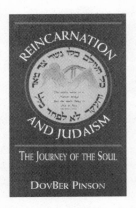

THE JOURNEY OF THE SOUL

DOVBER PINSON

REINCARNATION AND JUDAISM:
The Journey of the Soul
DovBer Pinson
0-7657-6064-9, $30.00

Reincarnation and Judaism: The Journey of the Soul is a comprehensive look at the intriguing concept of reincarnation as taught by the masters of Kabbalah and as analyzed by major Jewish thinkers throughout history. Rabbi DovBer Pinson, born and raised in a hasidic family and immersed in the study of Jewish mystical thought, has made a thorough search of Jewish teachings in order to present his readers with a rich and engaging study of life's most perplexing question: What happens after a person dies?

Rabbi Pinson looks carefully at questions such as: What is reincarnation? Why does it exist and how does it affect us in our lives? Do individuals have true "soul mates?" Is it possible to recall details from past lives? Do people reincarnate into animals? Does Judaism have a notion of "karma?" How do other cultures and faiths view reincarnation? What are the accurate and reliable sources in Judaism concerning reincarnation? What impact can belief in reincarnation have on an individual?

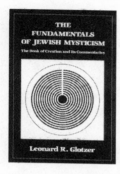

THE FUNDAMENTALS OF JEWISH MYSTICISM: The Book of Creation and Its Commentaries
Leonard R. Glotzer
0-07668-437-1, $40.00

The Fundamentals of Jewish Mysticism: The Book of Creation and Its Commentaries provides its readers with the background necessary to grasp the profound ideas of Jewish mystical theology. The modern student is often unable to crack open a kabbalistic text due to insufficient knowledge of the Hebrew language or a lack of basic information. Leonard R. Glotzer carefully guides the nonspecialist through a primary

text of Kabbalah, the result being not a book about Jewish mysticism, but a book of Kabbalah itself.

The structure of *The Fundamentals of Jewish Mysticism* is based on the author's translation of *Sefer Yetzirah*, known as *The Book of Creation*, one of the oldest and most important of kabbalistic texts. Many kabbalistic ideas appear for the first time in *The Book of Creation*, and it has served as a point of departure for all subsequent kabbalistic works.

MEDITATION AND KABBALAH
Aryeh Kaplan
1-56821-381-6, $50.00

"It is with great trepidation that one begins to write a work such as this, involving some of the most hidden mysteries of the Kabbalah. Many would question the wisdom and propriety of placing such information in a printed book, especially in an English translation. But so much misinformation has already been published that it is virtually imperative that an authentic, authoritative account be published. It is for this reason, as well as other reasons which I am bound by an oath to conceal, that the great living masters of Kabbalah have voiced their approval that such a book be published."

— Rabbi Aryeh Kaplan

the reader learns how Judaism conceived of the fate of the individual after death throughout Jewish history.

Among the topics discussed in this fascinating volume are heaven and hell, *Olam Ha-Ba* (The World to come), Gan Eden, resurrection of the dead, immortality of the soul, and divine judgement prior to death.

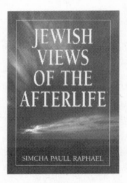

JEWISH VIEWS OF THE AFTERLIFE
Simcha Paull Raphael
1-56821-938-5, $40.00

In *Jewish Views of the Afterlife*, Simcha Paull Raphael guides the reader through 4,000 years of Jewish thought on the afterlife by investigating pertinent sacred texts produced in each era. Through a compilation of ideas found in the Bible, Apocrypha, rabbinic literature, medieval philosophy, medieval Midrash, Kabbalah, and Hasidism,

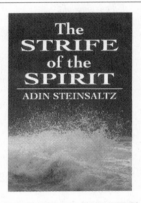

THE STRIFE OF THE SPIRIT
Adin Steinsaltz
1-56821-981-4, $30.00

In this long-awaited collection of Rabbi Adin Steinsaltz's essays, discourses, and interviews, the reader is offered a glimpse into the extraordinary mind of one of our generation's luminary rabbis.

The Strife of the Spirit explores such fundamental themes as the nature of the human soul, the path of the penitent, and the relationship between student and text. Those familiar with the work of Adin Steinsaltz will be delighted to find that many of his essays that have formerly been published in a variety of sources — as well as many unpublished works — are now together in one volume. Readers will encounter in this book a master teacher who, while deeply rooted in the most traditional form of Judaism, is extremely effective at shedding light on the meaning of Jewish existence for the newcomer.